SPIRIT –

RETURN INTO PARADISE

(A Spiritual Reconciliation with life)

Written by Spirit and Transcribed by

Brendan O'Callaghan

I.S.M. Publications

ISBN: 9798701697681

Cover design by: Brendan O'Callaghan

This book is dedicated to the future, in the hope its contents might inspire humanity to restore the earth to what it was so that it can again serve the purpose it was created for.

"The greatest fear is ignorance.

The greatest gift is the release from fear.

Wisdom is that gift.

Reject and remain fearfully ignorant.

Accept and become truly free."

'Spirit'

INTRODUCTION.

This book was transcribed during a short break in the transcription of the Spirit writings that are to be called, 'Spirit – Journey Through Embodiment'. Those writings were given in two parts, the first fifteen years and the rest of one's life. Spirit wanted to ensure that the first part was fully understood before the reader read the second part. These writings were to suggest how things might be should the understanding of humanity's Spiritual purpose be properly understood, and that awareness brought into practice and the world of humankind can once again become the Paradise it once was. It is hoped that this book will encourage the reader to look outside of the world as it is and to recognise the world as it could be. I hope that I have managed to transcribe Spirit's word to adequately convey the wonderful message of hope, love, and guidance.

The chapters might appear to be short. Each chapter contains what was given to me by the Spirit communicator at a sitting. As you read these words please understand this is how Spirit sees what is happening in the human world and wants to draw our attention too, so that we can develop an understanding of our dysfunctional ways and make the necessary changes to save humanity for its intended purpose.

In Love and Light,

Brendan O'Callaghan

CONTENTS.

CONTENTS contd.

CONTENTS contd.

COMMUNICATION AND THE LEVELS OF COMMUNICATION.

I have noticed that there are different groups of communicators for different topics and this group started by saying.... It has been a number of years since we used this machine in this manner. However, it will be like old times but new times also*, (the communicator referring to the computer).*

I remember your first communication with us; you were using a pen and paper. Your first communicator was Webb, me, then Sebastian, me, and then Essence, also me. Let me explain. The "level" of communication, the "level" of consciousness that the communication comes from, has to be compatible between the one receiving the communication and the one communicating. In your world when an adult communicates with a child, the adult needs to come to the level of the child. As the child matures, they increase in their capability to communicate, the communication becomes clearer and more imaginative topics can be discussed. Of course, between humankind and Spirit, there is such a gap in consciousness that the human has to use their imagination to be able to perceive our world. Can you perceive, for example, the universe and the details of it? You can't because it is beyond your perception. Can you imagine what it must be like to have that ability? Again, you can't and again it is because of the limited capacity of your human mental access. The first day we communicated I had to come to you as Webb, a fellow human, in order to attract your attention. I also had to have a verifiable history before I could get you to open your mind to what I had to tell you.

We have travelled a long road since then and now you have matured to the point where I can revert more into my true being. When you were in your previous consciousness you also had to go through a similar process and though you reached maturity as it was then you were only at the beginning of this journey you are presently on. It can take many incarnations to prepare for the work some choose to undertake.

Physically and mentally, in human body terms, what you are presently is an accumulation of all life's experiences to date. What you are Spiritually is a component of God, as is every Spirit. Each Spirit is complete and evolved to the point of now, and equally so. Unlike the human body, God cannot function in totality until all Spirits are present. Everything in creation has a Spirit and was possibly created by that Spirit to further the evolution of itself and thus of God. You might think of a Spirit being a separate entity, a unique being, yes you are unique but you aren't separate, you are an integral component of The Spirit. Here is where you need to use your imagination, a Spirit like The Spirit is omnipresent. In this case, though you are in this world as a human being you are a Spirit that is constantly and permanently connected to God, a component of the Supreme Spirit. The only part of you at this present time that has any negative potential is your ego-mind. If you like all the 'battles' between 'good' and 'evil' are merely illustrations of the conflicts that frequently occur in your world. When I refer to your world, I mean earth-consciousness. We also exist on earth and everywhere in the universe. You have heard of bi-location, that's a human term. In Spirit terms it is co-location, we are everywhere, in every dimension. For us, there is no particular place. Components of us might manifest in a particular place, for example, the component might choose to incarnate. While in an incarnate state it is not separated from the rest of its Spirit which is not separated from The Spirit. However, what can be separate is the ego. While incarnate the component Spirit and the ego of the body it occupies are inseparable. The ego tries to separate and can often fool itself into thinking it has, only to be pulled back to reality by its conscience, its Spirit.

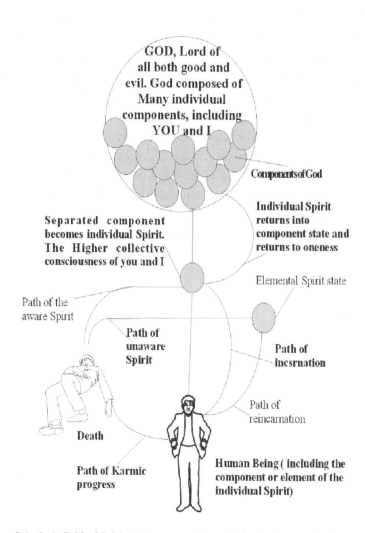

It is the individual Spirit, that component of God that seeks to evolve. The act of incarnation is a most positive act even for the Spirit that is in an elemental state. The State of unawareness is where positive aspects of negative experiences have not been assimilated by the incarnate Spirit. Each lifetime is for seeking fulfillment of Karmic purpose for that life. Death is the examination hall for that lifetime.

REINCARNATION.

I will refer you to an illustration we shared in the past, the one where we showed God as being composed of a multitude of components, and how the individual Spirit was one of those components. We also showed how the individual Spirit was composed of numerous components, and that each component had the opportunity to incarnate individually, this individual Spirit is the Spirit encased in human form. This is the Spirit that had chosen the journey through embodiment. It is linked to the individual Spirit and further linked directly to God. Even though it is far removed from God it still has a direct line to God and also, through this unity, is connected to all components that constitute God. Putting this into a universal context, with all components interlinked and interlinked with the individual Spirits, and the components of those Spirits, we can see how your Spirit is supported universally and interconnected with every aspect of the universe.

As your incarnate Spirit is intrinsically linked to your ego, every action your physical being takes reverberates throughout the universe. How you react to the consequences of your actions similarly is shared by all. These reverberations are felt on a human level as evil or goodness, your expression would call them vibes.

The negative vibrations that you might sense as foreboding are but your sensory system feeling the pressure of the approaching negativity of some collective reactions within the universe. Take for example how this disharmony that exists within your world these days is affecting the universe. At this time the counteractions of the spiritually conscious are being brought into focus and you will notice that the human population is coming to the point where this disharmony will no longer be tolerated.

There is no need for anyone to fear the outcome of the changes that are taking place as it would appear that progress is satisfactory. One needs to remember that the counteractions do not come solely from within the human population of the earth but come from the collective God-consciousness of the universe. To put things in perspective, the human consciousness without God-awareness is the lowest form of consciousness in the universe.

CONSIDER AND ADAPT.

It never ceases to amuse us, or amaze us, how the human mind filters and reacts to information it receives from whatever source. The human mind is selective to a degree that defies the logic it purports to possess. There is no accounting for how this message will be received, there is only the intent in which it is given that is pure. It needs to be constantly remembered that any message or teaching given by us is but our perspective and not in any way given for you to accept without applying your discernment and consideration. Please do not blindly accept and adopt, rather consider and adapt.

No information from this source is devised to manipulate or control you or to deliberately contradict your personal beliefs. You will often see that those who read these words will disagree and dismiss them without consideration. They will find them repugnant to their beliefs. If, however, they were to consider words given in this manner to be in addition to what they believe, and consider what portion of their existing beliefs are the beliefs of others that they have adopted, adopted in place of what they personally believed to be true, they will draw a fresh conclusion to what is their personal philosophy of their present life and arrive at the individual truths that are unique to themselves and the position in life they currently hold. Too many subscribe to belief and do not use their belief to find their truth. Too many are too lazy to venture further into the understanding of their lives and therefore accept any notion that they feel suits them and helps them avoid further seeking. This is why many accept the convenience of religion to satisfy the spiritual side of their nature. This latter way is why so many lay aside even religious practices because their religion lacks satisfaction.

It is often found to be more convenient to work for another than to work for one's self. Reconsider what we have just said, "to work for another than for one's self". Why would this offer any deep satisfaction? It is tantamount to selling one's life, and often not even to the highest bidder. In the employment of another, you are paid to do what they want you to do and not what you need to do. Look how many need to enjoy a hobby before they find satisfaction in life and to counterbalance the negative effect of the imposition of the needs of another upon themself. God gives you life for your use and spiritual benefit and not for you to sell on. Of course, you can work WITH another pursuing a mutual goal and sharing the mutual benefits, but how many employments are on this basis? Again, we stress that it is your life divinely provided for your spiritual benefit. You have also been given this life without conditions attached – therefore free will is yours to apply, however, remember that your life is constantly governed by the Law of Cause and Effect.

Through exercising free will you will make choices that are neither wise nor foolish but will always carry a consequence that will illustrate the appropriate lessons to be gained through the choices you have made. If the consequence is unfavourable then ensure you don't do it again and move on. It is never too late to do the right thing and change for the better, but the better of what? The better for your spiritual ease and comfort.

Spirit – Return into Paradise.

USING TIME.

The concept of time in human terms is unique to that species. Even within that species, it seems that time is a 'modern' concept and devised to order humanity. If one is to consider ancient calendars, they would only include such times as the time to sow and the time to harvest and would include a few other annual events such as anniversaries. The significances of these events were to the people and not to the corporations. There was no need for the subdivisions of the intervening times into weeks, days, hours, minutes or seconds.

These days timings are down to milliseconds. Have you ever pondered the necessity of this? Time has become your dictator. Yes, creation devised a certain order in the universe but humankind adapted that to its advantage, perhaps as a control system to maximise the commitment of the 'slave' to its 'master'. If one is to consider how this measurement of time determines one's actions, how so often there are "not enough hours in the day" in which to complete the tasks that are set for us, and how much time is set aside for the service of 'others'. How little time is set aside for self-service, how humankind has lost a sense of the importance of self, replacing 'self' with 'serve'. Of course, we acknowledge that there is a greater existence outside of ourselves but it does after all begin with the fundamental importance of human life, the journey of the Spirit through the world of incarnation. Yes, it might be found that one has chosen a life of servitude, but this does not imply that the service is at a cost to the server. All life must benefit the Spirit. We spoke of how humanity has been trained to sell itself to service. We spoke about how humankind has been enslaved through the manipulation into dependency. We spoke about how time has been devised down to a very tight schedule to manipulate the expenditure of human energy to the benefit of others who control and limit normal access to the facilities that the human being needs for its continued existence.

Humankind is on the brink of extinction as a consequence of the material greed of the few. The majority of humankind are enslaved and new births are but the production of fodder for the ruthless to use to further their material agenda. If one is to look into past societies, or even examine the structures that still exist within indigenous communities that have yet to be spoiled by those who seek to rule the lives of others, they would find Indigenous communities work as a unit, not as a collection of units working in competition with each other. There can however be an inter-community rivalry but these days there is war.

Humanities' thinking needs to return to its roots. God did not create this universe for the benefit of a few special people or families or races. God's creation was perfect for what God intended and then humankind took over and created chaos with its thinking of 'knowing best'. Humankind has an insatiable hunger for what it knows not and strives to feed that hunger at the cost of happiness. The universe is not something to be conquered, it is a paradise if only humankind could see the place that was created for it. A plague of sorts emerged out of what would be known geographically as Central Europe and has spread throughout the world. The corruption caused by this 'plague' died away but then returned. This return occurred from a different location but was more dangerous than its previous outbreak and still lingers on to this day. This plague is called socialisation and is affecting all areas of social structure. The major symptoms of this sickness are unhappiness, depression and an insatiable hunger for one knows not what.

Spirit – Return into Paradise.

THE UNIVERSE WAS CREATED FOR GOD.

The universe that God created was not for humankind, it was created for God and was a paradise. It was perfect. You will remember as a child playing with bits and pieces, and creating a fantasy from them. You would have made houses, and then added to that house to make it a home by adding more bits and pieces, and finally by adding a doll or two to make it a family home. As a child you would have played a variety of such games, in each case an expression of your creativity, an expression of your God-likeness, always drawing on your own 'imagination'. Or is it imagination or a memory, a Spirit memory of the act of creation being re-enacted but utilising the available bits and pieces and human consciousness as the building blocks?

As Spirit, you are part of that which created you, God. As a body, you are also a part of those who created you, your parents. Have you ever noticed children at play might often destroy their creation while others will preserve and protect their work? This could be an example of their inner conflict of their developing ego and their Spiritual awareness. The ego develops through praise or criticism. The praise will encourage the preservation whereas the criticism encourages the destruction or a need to hide the production from cynical or critical eyes. And then there is the other scenario where another child will dismantle or destroy the project of the other child, often re-enacting actions that have been imposed upon them. These situations are reflecting healthy or unhealthy developing egos. It seems that adult humans can still act out these emotions.

There are those who appreciate the creations of others, their art, their writing, their design etc., and then there are those who will criticise or in some way destroy their own creation or the creation of another. To take this topic a bit further, within the creation in which you exist at this time there are those who appreciate the creation of God and see its perfection and seek to preserve it. Then there are those who are cynical and critical of God's creation and can only see what they consider flaws or imperfections. The latter seek to destroy what is perfect and replace it with their synthesised version. Look at the world human population, how much artificially grown produce is now 'nourishing' humankind? How many are living in excesses? How do some progress in life and yet others remain static, and indeed how do they manifest progress There is even artificial intelligence? There is also artificially manipulated programming of human 'intelligence' through the misuse of communication systems. All this artificiality can only take place when God-consciousness is replaced by the rule of the 'masters' imposed on the 'slaves'. The ego is allowed to become the master and the Spirit becomes the slave. In these coming days, this will surely be reversed.

This can only happen by those who respect creation, and through God-consciousness express their desire to preserve perfection and will reject the overtures of their fellow humans to support and indulge their futile processed and artificial offerings.

It will be necessary that supply will meet the demand, and the demand will be for God-ness, and for the provisions that are God-given through God's creation and the spiritual awareness of the producers producing in God's name, maybe under the brand name of 'God-given'.

At these times in your small part of the universe, it is a case where Paradise has been lost. Always in nature, nature will restore itself and should humankind be cooperative and God-conscious, then Paradise can and will be restored with the help of God.

Spirit – Return into Paradise.

GOOD AND EVIL.

"And what of good and evil?" you might ask. This is not a spiritual question, however, no matter how it is asked. Possibly you might think we are in denial regarding the existence of these extremes. We are well aware of these circumstances but would hasten to add that they only pertain to the world you live in and not to the world of Spirit. This is why we say it is not a spiritual question.

God, the supreme Spirit, cannot create anything bad or evil. No aspect of God can be referenced in this way, and as all Spirits are of God there are no evil Spirits. Humankind created evil behaviour, and religions, all of which are man-made, use this to generate further evil in the fear they cause amongst their followers. It is the unawareness of truth that enables this fear. The greatest fear is the fear of the unknown. In Spirit, there is no fear as all is known. Even the future contains no fear for us as we know that the Divine plan is for happiness and for developing awareness.

Faith offers little comfort. Belief offers little truth, hope is hopeless. Knowing is the answer. How does one get to know? Ask a question.

29

Religion tries to give answers to questions that haven't been asked. Remember one of the most difficult words a child asks is "why", a word seldom used by adults as they feel they as adults should know the answers. These people would rather remain in unawareness rather than announce they are ignorant. This is a typical ego scenario, too proud to admit they are not all-knowing, and will sometimes even create a lie to hide their ignorance behind. This can lead one into an evil situation, a situation that is contrary to the truth.

There are no evil Spirits nor are there so-called fallen angels. The term angel is another name for a messenger from God. Unfortunately, this term has now been given status and even had a hierarchy developed around it. This is how evil is created. God has many messengers. All are of equal standing, none are "favourites". None carry out the duties humankind has conferred upon them. They are messengers from God and equally will carry your message back to God. Of course, should you develop your awareness and God-consciousness you wouldn't need any messenger by any name. You, your real self and your Spirit are equal to all others, an equal part of God and of equal status to all others. If you can't see yourself as such then you are still equal but too unaware to see it.

When you "raise" your consciousness to God you are in communion with God. Take as an example when you spiritually meditate, mindfulness is not included in this, you allow your physical consciousness to relax and your ego to quieten and God can hear you. You feel the closeness of Love, often to the point of tearfulness. You feel the beauty, the peace and the un-earthliness of Spiritual Consciousness. All negativity is outside of you. You might even feel a connectedness to, and equality with everything.

BEING FREE OF EGO.

Spirituality is another way of saying that your Spirit is free of the control of your ego. Unfortunately, this awareness is difficult to achieve while still embodied. Your ego is controlled by what are considered to be social norms. Your social system is largely based on the foundation laid down by the Roman Empire. It is a system intrinsically linked to the religion of Christianity and almost inseparable from what is truly 'natural'.

The Roman system was constantly feeding the empire through the empire, to make the system work for the benefit of the empire. To give the empire a face they had to have a human as a leader. This leader had no power of their own, they only had the power that was given to them. This conferring of power did not come without conditions and was dependent on the senate for instructions as to how it could be used. We are aware that the system was far more complex than we are stating, however, this exercise does not require that detail.

This system persists to this day in what is called Western Society. Take the example of a large company whose founder is no longer in that world, the founder's place has been taken by a piece of paper, a document, and this is now what controls the company. In a Christian sense, this document is the Bible. How authentic is this document? Not very much, and yet so many are controlled by it. Its influence on the legal systems of the Western World has been used, as in its past, to instigate laws that are imposed on the individual thus enslaving them. There is no freedom in the Western System, there is no freedom in any religion. How can one be free and yet have to conform to rules and regulations that have no direct bearing on their day-to-day existence?

You wake every day to what you have to do on that day. How much of this 'have to do' is you doing for yourself? You have to get up for work, you have to have a substantial breakfast so you have the energy to work. After work, you have to go home and you have to have your evening meal to restore expended energy. You have to sleep to restore your body to be fit to work, and so the pattern goes on and on. So many 'have to's', and all for somebody else, possibly even for a piece of paper. And then on the seventh day you rest, the one day for God. Even then this day makes demands on you, religious demands, and not even for the aspect of God that lives inside you. Humankind is so cruel to itself.

Wherein then is there any freedom in the lifestyle determined by your society. Humankind has sold itself into slavery. Even the slave owners are enslaved to the system that is of their own making. There is no freedom in that consciousness. But there is a solution.

PRAYERS FOR AVOIDANCE.

Rest assured we will get to the solution though only through you developing a greater understanding of the way of Spirit and becoming a willing participant in the process. Too often we encounter the entreaties of the unaware. If one were in your world, there would be no system that could handle the volume. This flow is a representation of the number of people living in a state of physical consciousness and not taking responsibility for what is theirs, their Spirit.

When we stated that there is a solution the human mind sought the 'quick fix', the patch that would solve everything. At this stage, there is no 'quick fix'. We have been drawing your attention to the way your society has been created and operates. Basically, the structure of your society is a series of 'quick fixes' with no one taking any responsibility for creating the problems in the first place. It's but a series of temporary repairs, one on top of the other. Things have gone too far to take any more temporary repairs, only replacement can correct this downward spiral. This is why we state it will take time.

So many feel that prayer is sufficient. Prayer would help but can only help when prayed properly. Too many prayers are what could be called 'avoidance' prayers. "Please God change the world". God created the universe but humankind created the world, therefore it is up to humankind to make the changes. But God will always be there to help. Why not pray, "God help me to do my part in changing the world"? Do you t hunk you would have the authenticity to play your part? Do you think you can afford the energy? Do you think you can afford the time? Do you think you can make a change in your life? Now you can see why we predict it will take a long time.

There are many just like you, who hesitate at the first hurdle. We said that this is a process, and will require your participation to complete it. The reason you are reading these words is that you are aware that there is a problem. Unfortunately, humankind is only seeing who to blame and not to correct the problem. We are taking this opportunity to let you know we know.

By these words we have changed your considerations into a new direction, that is if you have continued to stay with us this long. The good news is that those who have, have shown they want to be part of the process and though apprehensive are still interested. When one ventures into the unknown it is a difficult task when unsupported and even against all advice. For the average western socialised human, the area of spirituality, and again we would stress true spirituality, to venture into the morass of confusion that has been created around this topic, is certainly a daunting task. To enter a maze without the benefit of oversight would be a good analogy. However, this is not the case here. We have oversight and will ensure your safety and provide the guidance, you in your world and we in ours.

Having absorbed this information, you have taken the first step. To agree, and even better, to seek the necessary changes in you and your life, is the most difficult step taken. From this point, you become one of the many channels for change. You must become aware of your feelings and act on them. Never say yes or no just because it is socially or religiously accepted nor answer without seeing how you feel about it first. Look to the child for guidance on this, and their stubbornness in resisting the demands for them to override their feelings. In another communication, we have written about 'Spirit - A Journey through Embodiment'. In those communications, we have come to the point where these communications become important. The changes we seek humankind to make will be so important to the developing Spirit and child referred to in the other communication, that it will change their future, into a better future for them. We will be continuing the other communications after this current phase of these words. We are so please we are finally being listened to and change is about. No more patches.

Spirit – Return into Paradise.

THE FUTURE IS BRIGHT.

Believe it or not, the future is bright, but at this time not for humankind. Humankind has become so conditioned to only expect the worst and have therefore removed the potential of the 'silver lining' that every dark cloud was supposed to have. We have talked about the non-existence of evil as an external demonic state and this idea is so much part of the 'scare tactics' of controllers, whether it be through politics or religion, or 'slave-drivers'. All negativity exists only as a part of the human consciousness, as does positivity. We have spoken before as to how negativity requires no invitation whereas positivity does. We have also spoken of the conflict between the two consciousnesses of egoism and spirituality.

It is interesting to note that there is evidence of this conflict that is very obvious. When a discussion becomes an argument notice how there is an aggressive and a passive participation. The aggressiveness comes from the ego-consciousness and will not be satisfied until it is declared the winner, or failing that will blame circumstances not being in their favour. The passiveness comes from the Spirit-consciousness and doesn't need to win. The Spirit-consciousness will have love, compassion and understanding for the aggressor and will show patience. Sometimes it is very difficult, because of compassion, to allow the aggressor to protect their ignorance, but it is, however, necessary to also protect one's truth and perhaps 'beg to differ', and or walk away. Some aggressors will agree to differ, but will still need to assert that they are 'still right'.

The passive will often have to endure insinuations of all sorts of conditions being attached to them such as they are arrogant, close-minded, stupid etc, but this is the aggressor's ego attacking the ego of the passive. These labels will have no effect on the spiritual consciousness but consideration needs to be given to the welfare of the passive, and they might find they need to calm their ego.

The human ego is so similar to the animal instincts that have been excited in the domestic pets humans have. Depending on how the pet is treated by its 'owner' during its upbringing it will show aggressive or passive tendencies, no matter what the species of pet it may be. So too with human animals, their egos will reflect how they were treated during their upbringing. This can be noted within the different communities throughout the world, some are aggressive and some are passive; some constantly looking for a battle and some are content to be just left alone. Interestingly, most aggression comes from so-called religious countries, especially where there is religious extremism. Aggression is always negative; in extremes, it can be seen as evil. The aggressor will never take responsibility for their behaviour. In war, there is a mitigating term for the murder of innocents, it is called collateral damage. In society, there is a mitigating term for a murderer, they are called a soldier.

All aggression comes from ego-consciousness with aggression termed evil purporting to come from the devil. As humankind is created by God, so the devil is created by humankind. Evil 'Spirits' are but ignorant human souls, the souls of those bodies who lived in a state of ego-consciousness and whose bodies have created such a negative state, that their Spirit sought their removal from an earth existence. The Spirit cannot divest itself of the soul until such time as it can be 'deactivated' as it will still have such a strong sense of itself it will not 'die'. We have spoken before of the Spirit/soul connection, in the book 'Spirit – Releasing the Light Within', The Spirit is such a benign being with no time, so it is prepared to wait for the education of the soul into the awareness that will allow the soul to rest in peace for all eternity.

The Spirit does not feel the torture the soul subjects itself to. There is no hell as such, just the existence of a state where ignorant souls gather to console one another, often by feeding each other's unawareness. While in this state they can also 'see' what is going on in the physical world and can influence vulnerable minds into unfavourable, negative, or even evil behaviour. These souls themselves cannot affect those in the physical world but can influence embodied egos to do their bidding. The most vulnerable are those who are easily influenced. Every human whose spirituality is undeveloped, or underdeveloped is vulnerable. Every human who considers their ego before their Spirit is vulnerable. The most common manifestation of this vulnerability is the addiction to influence of any sort, including religion. When one puts their dependency outside of themselves for any reason, they become vulnerable. Some might depend on the fact they can use tobacco to demonstrate they are 'big enough' to smoke. Others will have dependencies on other, more influencing substances. It is the invitation the unaware gives to the negativity that makes them more open to greater negative actions, even down to the surrender of their own peace and happiness and indeed the peace and happiness of all they encounter are invited in. Such is the soul-destroying nature of dependency. On the bright side, all will sooner or later be unified in the One God.

THE END OF THE WORLD AS YOU KNOW IT?

You will be aware of the many strange happenings occurring in your world. This is but the end of the world as you know it. The ways of Humankind will bring about this. It will not be an ending with death and destruction. The fact we announce the end of your world lights up all the negative fears that have been instilled into the human psyche. God's messages never invoke fear, though they can provoke the fears that are within Humankind.

This is good news we bring as there are wonderful changes about. Take for example how vulnerable your society is. What would happen if simply money became worthless? Many indigenous societies still have the knowledge to enable life to continue without it, but Western Society doesn't, and yet life will continue on, and on. Think of what a wonderful world that would be. No rich or poor? No doubt you would have those who would try and reinvent the monetary system and those who would seek to help them, but money would be worthless and to try and reinvent it would be to invent worthlessness. An alternative would have to be sought. As we said the indigenous people will be the salvation of Humankind, not God but God's people, those whom society has tried to suppress.

Do you still fear the 'end'? Fear has a great chance of succeeding, as it has already got such a strong foothold in society. Even the fear of the very rich drives them to accumulate more in case they haven't enough. This is why the poor are in a better place and they are accustomed to having little if any. We use money purely as an example, to illustrate how dependent you have become on pieces of paper. Perhaps you are working for a piece of paper and get paid a piece of paper but you cannot nourish yourself or your family on pieces of paper. You have to convert the pieces into food. So why not just grow food yourself? It is the most uncomplicated job to do and the most rewarding, and the most natural thing to do. Dependency is so crippling to the nature of Humankind. How can anyone have time to even consider their relationship with God. There is that word again, time.

Time well spent yields proof of who you are. In Spirit, we measure time in sequences of cause and effect. In the example of growing your own food, you effectively reduce your dependency on others. The work you do can be more fulfilling for you. The energy you expended will provide you with at least enough, and often with abundance. As with all examples they are just that, an example. Do not rush out and begin growing your own food just because we used it as an example. There are those within every community that are food growers. They can grow the food for themselves and share their abundance with the rest. All have a particular ability and it is for them to find it and use it for independence's sake, whilst also sharing it with others around them. Like these writings are directly aimed at Brendan, as this is his forte to transcribe them and it is for him to share the abundance of words from us, with those around him and for other readers to share them also with those around them. If not these actual words, then the words that come to your mind as a consequence of reading these. Share and show you care. God is everywhere but difficult to find until you enter the domain of God-consciousness.

Spirit – Return into Paradise.

LIVING A LIFE.

To live one's life in a <u>total</u> state of God-consciousness is to not live any life at all. You are incarnate and have life for a reason. You are who you are, first and foremost a Spirit, but a Spirit <u>with</u> a body and a soul. It is impossible for a Spirit to manifest in your world otherwise.

Every living component in the physical world is there with these three separate but interlinked parts, and we stress everything, even the soil, the sand, the stones and rocks, everything. All of the universe is imbued with the Spirit of its creator. Everything that Humankind creates is also imbued with the energy of its human creator at the time of its creation. If one is to consider the simple tasks, such as creating a meal and go back to the source of the production of the ingredients, we can see the complexity of energies that coexist, including the existence of the Divine essence. Yes, the producer is just that a producer but the source of the ingredients of the producers' production is the Divine Creator. This is similar to two people producing a child. They create the circumstances to provide a Spirit, a Divine Being, the facilities for it to manifest in your world. They provide the body.

We know that, to your mind, our words on this might appear cold and clinical, but rest assured we are Love and can only describe the process from our perspective and not include the emotions a human might attach to it. We are from a very different consciousness than yours. We celebrate the death of the body, whereas you mourn death. To us physical death is the release of our loved one from the difficult environs of earth life, surely that is worth celebrating? Would you not celebrate the release of a fellow human from austere captivity? In the case of human reproduction, humans supply the biology as per God's creation, but God supplies the life energy, through the incarnating Spirit. This same life energy is that present in every living thing. This Energy is the life energy and, in the ingredients being used in the preparation of our meal, a component of the food being processed into a meal. These ingredients will also include all the input energies of those who produced them and even the energies picked from the environment around them as they grew.

In many productions, the attitude of the producer is reflected in the quality of the product. Let us look for a moment at the attitude of the producer. Are they vocationally suited to be doing what they are doing? Do they love what they do? What is their real motivation to do what they are doing? Are they working alone or do they employ others or share the workload with others? If the latter then we need to see what the attitudes of the others are, as their energy input is also present in the finished product. If the answer to any of the questions suggests other than love and happiness then the effect on the product will not be favourable. You have a saying in your world about rotten apples in barrels. You will have experienced the difference between 'having to' and 'wanting to' and 'needing to'. 'Having to' often attracts resentment, 'wanting to' attracts control and dissatisfaction, and 'needing to' attracts fulfilment. You see, needs are the requirements of Spirit, whereas the other two are solely to do with the ego and its hunger.

We have only discussed the production of the ingredients to be used by the producer of the meal. It is the cook who carries the next stage of preparation. What is their attitude? The same criterion applies. They need to ensure they include the best ingredients they can. In the preparation of the ingredients for inclusion in their menu they can, should they be aware, cancel out or dispel, or dilute any negativity that might be attached to any ingredient. The core and most spiritually nutritious component in the ingredient is its life energy, its spiritual energy. It is its soul energy that carries any contaminating negative energy, while its body energy provides the nutrition your body needs. The final meal is presented to the consumer. Again, attitude is important. The consumer needs to be aware of all that went into the presentation in front of them, from the act of God in creating the Spirit and body of each component, through the attitudes of those involved in the production of the component, to the graciousness of the cook who would also have left part of their energy in every mouthful to be consumed. A moment's reflection provides the opportunity for the consumer's love and appreciation to also be added to the food and would be tantamount to a blessing. The meal is now sacred and all who were involved are blessed. Of course, you will realise that if you were, yourself, with this awareness, the producer and the cook, would you not think it would be a most beautiful and fulfilling meal you could have, all by the grace of God.

Spirit – Return into Paradise.

48

ALL IS ALWAYS IN GOD'S HANDS.

There is a feeling of trepidation, yet there is no need to worry or even to be concerned. All is always in God's hands, no matter who might claim otherwise. Even those doing 'bad deeds' are doing so of their own free will which is God-given, but the deed is also subject to the Law of Cause and Effect, which is also God-given. The Law of Cause and Effect is also the 'tool' which is used for all creation. It is constantly being used by everything that is of creation and for showing humankind the consequences of its action, both good and bad. This is why we can assert that "All is always in God's hands".

God-given free will enables the expansion of spiritual awareness, and the Law of Cause and Effect adjudicates and informs humankind of the appropriateness of its actions. Some call this law Karma, but see Karma as the punishment or rewarding of 'good' or 'bad' deeds, and for these rewards or punishments to be presented sometime in the future. This latter concept is not as it is. There is a law that says 'every action has an equal and opposite reaction'. When this law is correctly utilised and understood it is possible to have a rewarding or punishing experience in the 'now'. The weakness of humankind, whilst acknowledging these laws, is to expect to avoid them and all consequences and to feel they are above the laws. As God is the creator and applier of these laws, which incidentally require no supervision, they are perfect and complete. Not even God is free of their application. After all, they are the building blocks of continuous creation and spiritual growth.

Be aware of what you choose to do and be prepared for the consequence. Isn't it strange that our last comment should give a feeling of fear and apprehension? To one spiritually aware, however, it will give a feeling of excitement. Remember how a child feels when it is about to see the outcome of its creation, it feels excitement. What then has happened to that child that it loses that excitement and replaces it with apprehension? It has become socialised. Remember how as a child it has no fear, and then it becomes afraid. Where did that fear come from? There are of course exceptions to every generalisation. One can have a child with strong spiritual awareness who will be born with an inherited fear from its parent. Many happenings occur during its gestation period, where the external happenings in the environment that surrounds the pregnancy, affect the psychology of the developing child. The fears the mother experiences, whether with or without reason, can be transmitted to the developing child within the womb. The developing child cannot rationalise the fear and can therefore be born with it. Then there is also the unsupported awareness the child possesses at its birth, its spiritual awareness.

If one can understand, no Spirit has fear. The human is the only species that creates fear. Most fear is generated by human conversation, directly or indirectly. During its gestation the child, though it cannot 'hear' as such, can react to sounds and especially to 'feelings' around it. The mother who fails to feel supported in her pregnancy and subsequent birth will often suffer apprehension that, with the 'help' of her fellow's negativity, will develop into a fear, a fear that will be transmitted to the child who will then be born knowing fear. The parenting this child receives will then relieve it of this fear or will compound it. Unfortunately, due to the lack of spiritual awareness in its parenting, the result will be that fear will become a part of its life, often for its lifetime. Only God-consciousness can relieve that fear.

Spirit – Return into Paradise.

GET,

'TO KNOW AND TO SEE GOD'.

The God-consciousness that we refer to is not merely being aware that there is a God, not just being aware of the teachings about God-consciousness, but being aware of the Godliness that is within every aspect of God's creation, and the respect that is due to that Spirit, that manifestation of God on earth. Many seem to think that it is sufficient to belong to this or that religion, that it is sufficient to align themselves to some teacher or guru or leader and follow them. This is not the case. 'Fervent' believers merely follow and seldom embrace the truth. God is within each and every part of God's creation. Until this is understood no one can even say they believe in God.

The purpose of human life is so that the ego, the body and the mind, get to "know and to see God". The way humans currently lead their life would make this to be an impossibility. Humans treat life as if it is a chore and complain about its harshness, sooner than to recognise the possibilities and potentials, that life holds, for happiness and fulfilment. Many cannot eat the food that God provides without polluting it with harmful poisons, sauces and garnishes, in an attempt to flavour out its natural taste and benefits. Many foods that humans indulge in are only nicely flavoured poisons. Even the flavourings themselves often contain poison. The water provided through God's creation for you to drink is poisoned before you are allowed to drink it, unless you harvest the water yourself. One might be inclined to think that we are advocating a particular dietary regime, but we are not. What we are advocating is a food regime that is based on God-given foods, foods that require no special sauces or flavourings that are but creations of the food industry. The skill of proper blending of God foods has been lost to commercialism and industry. The time needed to produce God foods in a Godly manner has been lost to those companies and industries who convert the Godliness in the food into financial wealth rather than spiritual nourishment. Commercially processed food is in the main Godless food, and often nutritionally deficient also. It is a filler, not a fulfiller.

We won't go into any actual process that your food goes through, but assure you it is not healthy. God is within all. In the case of those seeking to profit from God's presence, God retreats from them. God never leaves, as God cannot remove itself without bringing life with it. You have a saying, "Where there's life there's hope", and where there is God there is therefore hope. But what is this hope referring to? In spiritual terms, this hope is that one day all humankind will be one with God, and through God-consciousness. How will that happen, you might ask? Read back on what has already been written and become aware of its true content. Read beyond the words. Humankind must revert to being self-sufficient. It is good to be reliant and reliable rather than dependent and dependable. It takes a very strong community to pull together.

The very way society is structured in your world these times is to create division rather than cohesion within the greater community of Humanity. Each community grouping by its very nature provides a unique culture of its own. Each unique culture offers a special aspect to provide happiness and harmony to the human population of your world. It would appear that this mutual cooperation between communities, each adding their uniqueness to society, poses a threat to those in power, or better to say those who have taken power from the people. By the way, happiness and harmony do not yield financial profit. So too does self-sufficiency pose a similar threat. Imagine a world where each and every individual human were self-sufficient. This was the way the world was for thousands of years. Now ask yourself the question, "What happened to disrupt this happiness and harmony"? The simple answer is that unhappiness was introduced by greed, and disharmony was introduced by the need to control. Remember 'control' was there already, but it was self-control guided by the Law of Cause and Effect. This law was devised by God, not only to provide the basis of continuous creation but for the guidance of all of creation, see how many are now guided by reward and punishment.

These words we give you are to help you be aware of what you have forgotten, denied, are blind to see, or just don't want to know for lazy or defensive reasons. Yes, no doubt you have your reasons but in truth are they truly reasonable. If you are to love one another then it must be without condition to be Divine. To provide for each other it must be in love. To care for one another also must be with love and without condition. Only then can there be happiness and harmony. All are equal, even "man and beast". Paradise is redeemable.

Spirit – Return into Paradise.

THE ROAD TO PARADISE.

The road to "hell" is well paved as it is constructed by materialism. This road is hard and straight with high banks on either side. It is well maintained and much used. But this road has its toll booths, not only at its beginning and its end but also has innumerable booths along its entire length. It's for those who are in a hurry to reach their goal, the goal of mythical success.

The road to paradise, however, meanders through lush green pastures, unfortunately, is less worn and therefore less distinct. It affords expansive views and has no tolls to be paid. It is paved with love and happiness. This is a road one would hope would never end as it gets better and better. This road is so smooth that one hardly realises they are moving forward to their destiny. It is the road to infinity, and to the infinite God. It is the road only the spiritual can travel.

Viewed from the earthly perspective, the material road is the obvious choice, it is clearly mapped out for you by the society to which you have been sold into by your upbringing. You have been trained to take that road and discouraged from taking any other. Now we have drawn your attention to this matter you will begin to realise that indeed there is always another way. Initially, your ego consciousness will refuse to see it, and with the assistance of those similarly unaware acquaintances, you will have your closed thinking endorsed, and become blind to any opportunity of there being an alternative way and you succumb to the "have to", and the "one and only". Take the example that is often encountered in life, your need to travel to a far off destination. The question is posed, do you take the highway or the byway? The factor of time comes into the equation, what time do you have to arrive at your destination? And then the question we would put to you is, do you even know where your destination is? The more modern the road the faster it will be, but is the vehicle you travel in built for such a speedy road, will it last the journey? Is it fit for the purpose your narrow thinking seeks to subject it to?

Your body is not designed for such stress and pressure and though it might take you to where you think you need to go; it will not take you to your true destination. Your body will become so decrepit that you will seek to abandon it. Let us look at this example. You will see how your physical being and its mind will become entrapped by the society it is born into, a society that has its own agenda for all its participants. This agenda is only for the preservation of the society and does not cater for the individual, especially those who might not 'fit in' to its plan; the individual who has other ideas, who doesn't conform, who says 'no' when the system wants 'yes'. You will notice that these wonderful individuals are becoming more common and for the system are more problematical.

The system is faltering and cannot cater for the diverse needs that these individuals present. For the last one hundred or so of your years there has been a silent revolution, a hidden revolution with individuals becoming incensed with the incarceration of their behaviour, not being allowed to be themselves but constantly forced to be who society seeks them to be. They are controlled and conditioned. Society has developed a class system where there are 'boxes' for certain sectors of society to be placed in and catered for. You have the upper, middle, and lower classes. You have the upper-middle class and the working class. You have the white-collar worker. There are now so many categories that you can be placed into, and should you find yourself totally outside all categories you are titled disabled. The label disabled only shows that the system does not cater for these people, and doesn't know how to incorporate them into its structure. There is nothing wrong with them except in society's eyes.

Allow yourself to think about which box you are in and then ask yourself is this really who you are, or is this definition of you just as society wants you to see yourself, and for you to take your place within it? If you don't conform, if you are to be truly yourself, society will probably deem you to be anti-social and out of control. In other words, you are your own person. You have your pets, animals that you acquire and domesticate. They are thought how to behave so that they can fit into your way of life. You make them dependant on you for everything, and when you don't need them you park them at your convenience. When they become inconvenient you dispose of them. You have created your own miniature society. You have presented yourself to them as their God, much the same as your society presents you with so many 'gods', the high-ranking politicians, the executives of industry, the religious leaders who claim to have direct contact with the Divine and are infallible.

Where then is your understanding to come from, where then can you see the one true God with so much to obscure your vision? The individual has a link to God that is clear and uncluttered without the dross of social conditioning. The individual can only survive through exercising their independence and self-sufficiency. It might need a certain austerity to be experienced as society will not condone its individuality, but the austerity will never outweigh the joy and benefits of freedom, both physically and especially spiritually.

THE EGO IS NURTURED BY THE SYSTEM.

We are not the 'kill joys'. It is not we who dictate how you should or should not lead the life you live. You have free will and the Divine right to make choices in your life. It is you who surrender these rights to others and it is this loss of freedom that 'kills joy'.

When a body is born, it is born in a state of strongly active spiritual consciousness. We have already stated that in some cases it might be born in a state of fear, due to issues during the pregnancy and delivery, but nonetheless, it will be spiritually conscious. It is easy to understand the vulnerability of this newly emerging being to the manipulations of society and the system. The newborn has a dependency on its fellow human beings for everything. It depends on its mother for nourishment, hygienic care, clothing etc. This is how God created humankind, every human possesses the instinct of caring for its young, naturally. All animals do, all creatures do. We have discussed at length how the newborn loses its sense of its spirituality as it grows further into its human form. We have discussed how the human ego is nurtured by the system but the Spirit is neglected. (These discussions referred to, take place in the partner publication, 'Spirit – A

61

Journey through Embodiment'). When the spiritually un-nurtured human faces out into the world it is totally at the mercy of the system and on the road to losing happiness and joy. It may think it is happy but with the absence of joy, it will be but an illusion.

How often you will hear people say, "I thought I was happy". An egotistical, material life is full of emptiness and is lacking in fulfilment. We have used food as an example of this. Food prepared and cooked in haste, eaten in haste, digested hastily, provides little in the way of nourishment and fulfilment and carries only bulk and problems into the body systems. Every action performed within the timescales provided by the human-made systems, that govern the actions of humankind needs to be recalibrated into God-time.

Humankind needs to rethink what it has done. It's had its industrial revolution and now needs to revolve again, but on this occasion to have a Spiritual revolution. This is possible without even taking to the streets in protest. There is a 'second coming' and it is coming now. We hope you feel the inspiration contained in these words, if you do then you are becoming part of the new way, the new world, a world spiritually created in harmony with God's creation, and not created to pander to the material greed of the few. To realise this spiritual awakening is to realise the inadequacies in the current provision, within the current social structures, of spiritual awareness and sustenance. Society has provided religious institutions to replace Spirit. Spirituality can never be institutionalised. A spiritual human being is one who is applying God's provisioning to its lifestyle and utilising all that God has provided for the betterment of its own life and therefore to the lives of fellow spiritual travellers. The knowledge of this has been lost, and therefore denied to the developing human mind during its childhood.

Many reading these words will have a pet animal. Some will treat that pet as one of the family. Even to feed it with a human family diet. They will teach the animal to do tricks and to behave in a way that satisfies the human. All this is done with no consideration given to the Spirit that is also part of the animal who is but a pet to the human. It must be remembered that everything in God's creation is imbued with the love of its Creator. Your pet is loving but also dependent, dependent because of your actions in socialising it into human ways.

The human way is now the material way, not God's way. Consider how you treat or would treat an animal pet. Now consider how you treat your fellow animals, human animals. Is there a similarity? Ask yourself this question, but do not answer it. If you have answered it, the answer comes from your ego and will be wrong and defensive of your ego self. The spiritual revolution is at hand. Ask yourself this question also, do you want to be part of it? Also ask yourself this question, on which side will you be? This latter is a trick question as there are no sides in a spiritual revolution, there is only unity.

Spirit – Return into Paradise.

LACK OF SPIRITUAL AWARENESS.

You might think we are being critical of the social system that humankind has created; we are not being so. What we are doing is pointing out the lack of spiritual awareness in its construct, and the disastrous effect this lacking is having on the welfare of, not only the whole human race but also on the other occupants of that planet and its environment. If this were to continue the earth will be joining the countless planets in the universe that are desolate and deserted, apparently devoid of any life. We say apparently because every part of this universe has life in some form, God is present everywhere. One could say where there is God there is life. This does not mean there is form. That a form is human does not mean it is alive, it may just be a corpse, a form that the Spirit has removed itself from. Eventually, it will crumble away and reform as the cells that could comprise another form such as the soil you walk upon. Even then you can see life in that soil or see the soil is dead and infertile.

Of course, you can re-energise everything, you have the expression, "Breath new life into it". Look at those who are, if you like 'dead on their feet', and consider the possible real meaning of this expression. In essence, it refers to people who have given their all to the project they are involved in. They are completely drained of all energy, including spiritual energy, though they are still alive. The only reason that they are still breathing is that their Spirit is still supporting their body in the hope that the ego will relinquish its grip, that the body will recover from the physical and mental exhaustion, and might have lost its resistance to the changes that need to take place for the spiritual goals to be achieved. This stage is most commonly observed in mental and/or physical illness. It is not the result of hard work, rather it is the result of hard 'thinking'. It is living through the ego and not through the Spirit, the body and the mind have exhausted themselves with a poor return.

Give love, get love, give labour get paid. Payment will only help in the purchase of the necessities of the body and mind, but can never purchase the necessities of the Spirit incarnate. These spiritual necessities are free to all and yet are priceless. The only ways they can be accessed are through awareness. We will use the analogy of food once again. Most of what you discard can be recycled into fresh produce. We said about the cells of the dead form being recycled into a new form. Sometimes the cells of the human form can be recycled to provide a form for future generations, new life can be breathed into them. Think of the story of Adam and Eve, the story of the creation of humankind, God took some soil and breathed life into it. Think of the potter who takes some clay and gives it a new and most useful form. All are in their own right creators of some form. What have you created in your lifetime? Was it created through love, to love? You will no doubt remember contributions you have made to society through 'love', but how often these contributions will have been through a sense of duty and not through love. Do you have a social conscience? Think how often this conscience clashes with your instinct, with your inner feelings, "I know I shouldn't be doing this but…". Social conscience is not there for guidance, it instructs. It is but an excuse for conforming to the pattern society demands of you.

Religious conscience is similarly used to manipulate your ego into supporting the religion. Social conscience is used to manipulate your ego into supporting society. Spirit doesn't have a conscience; it is pure love and can never do wrong. Spirit can never be manipulated therefore by either society or religion, though these latter still try to do so. This is why we stress the necessity of God-consciousness. If you have God-consciousness you will often find yourself in conflict with what are the accepted social and religious norms. This is one of the dilemmas presented to the evolving human and its evolving Spirit, the dilemma created by the conflict of the unaware ego and the aware Spirit.

Spirit – Return into Paradise.

INSIGHTS INTO LIFE.

It is our intention that we can provide you with insights into your life and these insights will enable you to find the Paradise that God created, not as it was but as it is. Have you ever noticed that you have lost the appreciation of simple things, simple foods, simple drinks, simple fun, etc? The simplicity that has been provided for the nurturing and nourishing of human life has been totally obscured by the veneer of well-being provided by the system that society has developed.

We referred to pet animals earlier and now we draw your attention to the fun, comfort, and enjoyment a dog gets from chewing a simple bone. How simple it is for them to enter into contentment. Watch a child get enjoyment from the simple things also, how their imagination brings them into a different consciousness where there is a wonderful world to be accessed. A simple piece of paper and a pencil can provide them with endless fun.

Watch children playing 'Mammy' and 'Daddy', this can be a painful experience when it is you they are emulating. It can be a very revealing experience when you realise what it is about you that they are portraying. Maybe it is your intolerance, your distance and disconnection, your difficulty with coping. Children have honesty; it is those that are supposed to care for them that teach them dishonesty. You will often see that tuition emerging from the play and interaction of children. On the one hand, you seek to provide a better life and a better way of life for your children, but instead, you inadvertently offer them the same, and possibly worse scenario for living. Life is becoming more complex and more difficult to live. The divisions between humankind are increasing. If you look at the recent history of the human race, in the social history, you will notice that there was an increasing division amongst the classes that comprised the population. Then there was war and suddenly the division decreased as all came together to face the common 'foe'. It became a one divide, 'them and us'.

Let us not fail to see it is still a division between two sides. It is still thought to be self-righteousness on both sides, where in fact it is a power struggle orchestrated from the epitome of human negativity. You look at the behaviour of other animals, dogs for example never wage war on an international scale. No other animal does, only the human-animal. It is the human-animal that turns other animals into fighters. It is only the human-animal that turns its own into fighting machines, trained to kill their fellow human. If one were to attend to their own business in cooperation with their fellows, why would there be the need for such power struggles?

Every fight is instigated by an outside negative influence, outside of the Spirit that is. It could be the negative influence of the ego, which is constantly seeking recognition and power. It could be the influence of the ego of another. It could be the influence of a substance that is being abused. It could be the influence of the collective negativity of the human race commonly referred to as the Devil. Children are exposed to this latter

70

influence without being shown how to recognise it or how to deal with it. They are only shown how to fear it and how to use it as an excuse for their inappropriate behaviour. Children are seldom taught to be responsible adults, never mind being taught to be responsible spiritual adults. We will not go into the causes for war at this time, but suggest that if the philosophy we are imparting were implemented there would be no war. War has no place in spiritual philosophy, nor in Paradise.

Allow yourself the luxury to dream of your idea of paradise. It will take some time to move past the conditioning of your upbringing and to see the simplicity of a world without stress and trouble and fear. If one is to address the basic needs of its corporal state, it will see simple it could be to achieve them. When you think of a holiday what do you think of? When you break it down it is usually only respite that you seek, you need to get 'away from it all' even just for a short while. You need to 'recharge the batteries' you feel. Why do you not also see the need to change your life so that you enjoy every day, and not rely on your 'two weeks in the sun' to placate the need for joy and happiness being in your life every day? Notice how you wake every morning thinking of what it is you have to do that day. Think of how you wake on the first morning of your holiday, and then remember how you awaken on the last day of your holiday. Think of how during your holiday you find it hard to entertain yourself and when you find that interest it is time to prepare to go home. Finally, ask yourself why does it have to be that way? Now think of paradise, what would satisfy you, what would give you joy?

Let us remind you again of the war years and how all people reunited as a community. Let you remember that the little plot of land could feed a family, how a dandelion, now considered a weed again, was an important part of the food chain, and the nettle too. Remember how instead of a flower you planted a vegetable, or if a flower it was an edible one. Remember how the chicken was a luxury to eat as the bird was also needed for its eggs. Remember how red meat was also a rarity, at best once a week. Food was rationed, but not the food you grew yourself. What a healthy lifestyle war gave you. It was that you would repair your garments rather than discard them. It was that you would repair rather than rebuild. It might have been a life without sophistication, but it was a life.

If you speak to those who lived through that austerity, asked them about the fun they may have had. Usually, they will still laugh at the memories of the simple fun they had, whereas history only records the misery. The fun that was had is always about the wonderful human interaction that took place when the community came together. Isn't it such a shame that it took a war to cause that? Isn't it a shame that it takes an illness to cause one to appreciate life? Isn't it a shame that it takes death to cause one to appreciate God?

APPROPRIATE CHOICES.

Have you ever thought about time? We know we have addressed this previously but at this point, we want again to highlight an issue regarding its relevance in controlling or being used to control your life and your activities in that life. If we were to mention a time and date in your life you will automatically relate to an event that occurred then. You will say that was when such and such happened. If we were to refer to the event, however, you will not automatically refer to the time and date. Does this not suggest that the event is more important than time?

Humankind has become preoccupied with measured time. Irrespective of time, what else led you to the event? In one word, circumstance. Circumstance, the dictionary tells you, "is a fact or condition connected with or relevant to an event or action". The circumstances come about due to choices you have made leading you to an event that is a marker of where your life is going, as a result of those choices. Remember, we have said nothing is good or bad. These definitions only relate to the suitability of your choice being favourable to your needs, and not to your wants. You need to know if your choices are appropriate to you in your life journey, and the 'you' we refer to is you your Spirit. It might appear that the decision you made was unfavourable to your spiritual needs even though it might have been a want of your ego. Then again it might have been favourable to your spiritual needs and your ego, thus showing a harmony of both these aspects of your being.

It could be said that the bad event in your life was really when you satisfied your ego impulses and overrode your spiritual instincts, even though you got a certain comfort from it, but were left with an emptiness. It could be called, "a hollow victory" of ego over Spirit. In recognising these scenarios, you will be more discernible in the choices you are making and in turn find that life is not always a battle to 'do the right thing'. If you like life is a series of possibilities being presented to you to bring you to your goal.

We spoke of the simplicity of life, humankind with its subservience to the social system makes it complex. It is naïve to think that God would have created the earth, and then created the human species to dwell there, and made no provision for the ability of that species to survive. The system created by God appears to function for every other species but in your society, it seems to fail humankind. Do you never question why this is? Humankind by its nature is not destructive and yet it appears to be destroying its environment and creating the means of its own extinction, while 'praising the Lord'. What a folly, what a dilemma. However, help is on hand but humankind needs to listen. Each individual has a responsibility, firstly to themselves, to stop what they are doing and to look and listen to what their world is saying to them. Look to an understanding of the Law of Cause and Effect to guide you. Avoid labelling anything as being intrinsically good or bad, good or evil, God or Satan. Avoid blaming anybody, thing or circumstance. Accept everything as it is, guidance along your chosen path, and how you feel will give you the response to turn another way or maintain your direction.

There are many factors introduced into human life that are causing confusion. Humankind is being 'trained' by its society to dress in a certain way, eat in a certain way, socialise in a certain way etc. All these certain ways are to suit the system and not necessarily the individual. Everything you have, everything you do is at the behest of the system, even in how you are told how you should wield your personal, God-given, free will and power. You are cajoled into surrendering to the system. If you continue to behave in this unnatural way your life will be spiritually worthless.

Take responsibility for yourself. This does not mean you need to suffer. "Isn't life all about suffering", you will often hear stated. Suffering is about being in, the wrong place, at the wrong time, and doing the wrong things. If you are suffering in life, then now you know why. That state certainly isn't Paradise. If you are suffering then ask yourself why, and don't make excuses or blame anyone else or anything. Above all else don't answer your own question. Take it that as you don't have the answer to hand is the reason you asked. You do have the answer but it has been hidden by all the conditioning you have accepted from the system. Life will remind you of the answer, whereas the system will distract you with the statement we used earlier, "Isn't life all about suffering".

Finally, for this day we will say to you to keep within the boundaries of your own life and not impose on the boundaries of the lives of others. Find how self-sufficient you are and note that your inefficiencies are due to your own laziness and responsibility to yourself. Approve of who you are and don't measure yourself against others. Appreciate you are perfect, should you choose to see it. You are a 'stand-alone' being once you are altogether, Mind, Body and most importantly Spirit.

SYNOPSIS.

To synopsise what we have already written, first and foremost you are Spirit; you are a Spirit on a mission to evolve; you are part of the evolving perfection that is also known as God; your destiny is in infinity; your sojourn on earth is but a brief period in your particular role; that you are in the ever-present now; that at this time you are contained within a body and a soul; that your body's ancestry has only to do with your body and nothing to do with the past of your Spirit; your body is solely a transport system chosen for its particular peculiarities, and at this time you are being subjected to wiles of a dysfunctional human-created, or perhaps a better term might be generated, social system. To some, these might seem to be critical statements, though that is not our intention. We intend to draw your attention to the circumstances your ego is subjecting your Spirit to. Our intention is to assist you in becoming aware of who you truly are and why you are in that world at this time.

As this dissertation is for general distribution we can only therefore generalise, and not be specific to any one individual. You will appreciate that this would be a difficult task were we not here on behalf of the Divine. God will guide us as God will guide you. We intend that these words will generate an awareness in you that will cause you to question all that has been in your life up to now. However, we hope you will take cognisance of what has already been written and that you will take full responsibility for all that has happened, that it has been through your choices, and that you will take full responsibility for having made them, and responsibility for the consequences. No one else is in any way responsible.

We know that this will be difficult for you to accept in many cases. It is important to note that should you disagree with us; it will be that you are in denial of what is true and have a closed mind. We are not offering these words to you for you to accept without question. We are not offering these words as anything other than our truth. We are offering these words as a hypothesis, as a framework on which you will build your own personal truth. The system has implanted the thinking process that will reject any viewpoint that does not suit its formula for control. You are a victim of the propaganda of the system. You are conditioned to react negatively to positivity.

Before you feel the impulse to react, pause a moment and see what you are contemplating doing. Why should you not allow the viewpoint of others? Why does it always have to be your view or no view? Is it even your view or is it the viewpoint of another that you are allowing to close your mind to fresh ideas or other views? Has a child's viewpoint never opened your memory of forgotten perspectives? The struggle you are experiencing with these words is but the struggle in your mind to weigh belief against the truth. We have no reason to impart anything but the truth, and indeed it is not within our power to do anything else, as in our world there are no lies. Would you believe us if we told you that in your world also there are no lies, only illusion and delusion? Until you can accept what is, you will continue to be deluded and suffer illusion, and thus controlled by the system you have accepted to live by.

Please do not feel disheartened or despondent. Things aren't meant to be any different than they are. They are as they are because of the misplaced trust in others, and trust not placed in yourself. You are carrying the burden of the responsibilities of the thinking and choices of others, but only because you have chosen to do so. Irrespective of the behaviour of others you have a duty to yourself, and only then to those you carry responsibility for. These latter responsibilities should never be permanent, your needs should always take precedent.

This must never be seen as selfish. Negative selfishness is entirely different, this is self-preservation so that you can fulfil your role in this life. Nobody comes to be a sacrificial victim, every life has a purpose. It's up to you to live yours. At this time in these writings, we are turning the corner into a better future but only should you choose to heed these words, consider them, and then implement the truth you discover through them. It is always up to you, and with the grace of God.

Spirit – Return into Paradise.

FEAR IS THE PRODUCT OF HUMANITY BEING ENGROSSED IN ITS NEGATIVITY.

So, it is all up to you. It is your life, your responsibility, your choice, no matter who or what seeks to impose their will or way upon you. No state or religion has authority over you unless you allow it. How then is it that these authorities appear to have that control? You are controlled through your dependencies. You rely on the state to support your body and the church to support your Spirit, yet you, and you alone 'suffer' the consequences. The 'clever' way these authorities took over the control of your life is nothing short of criminal. You were born free and almost immediately registered into the state, Christianised through baptism, and so inadvertently became the property of the church and state. You no longer had access to the Divine Rights provided by God. God created the earth, but humankind created the world it lives in, and the faith it believes in. It is no longer, "In God we trust", we close out God's light and switch on the electricity.

When you become aware of this there is no going back. One can never become unaware, but you can forget or suppress awareness. In the majority of western humanity, this latter is the case. Your vision of God has been obscured by the negative manipulation of truth, substituting belief for truth, and the limitations on your freedoms by the forced removal of your Divine rights through submitting you to the control of the state. You are no longer allowed to have access to God-given land without a permit, the state has claimed it all for its own and then sold it to those who had the means to purchase it. The title you sign is an agreement with the state, not with God. This is what you sign up for when your arrival into that world is registered.

So what can you do about that you may ask? You can realign yourself to God, and go about living your life God's way. We do realise how difficult this might sound; we know that you cannot relinquish your dependency on the state. Your 'dependency' on the church, however, is easy to release. Your spiritual existence depends on you taking responsibility for being an independent spiritual being and free from the chains of the laws of the church. If one were to fully understand the fundamental law, the Law of Cause and Effect, and live by the guidance that law affords you, you would access Paradise while still on Earth.

To follow this guidance, you will of necessity give this Law precedence over any human-made laws, and exercise your God-given rights. As we have said before, humankind needs to take responsibility for who they are and behave accordingly. Life has become more important than truth. Life has become more important than living. Which is preferable, to live a short and fulfilled life or to live a long and empty life? The answer is simple, incarnate life has a limited duration. It has a beginning at birth and termination at death. The time in between these two is the time required for you, the Spirit, to achieve its purpose for incarnating. The western philosophy of these times does not seem to be aware of this and thus seeks to control the lifespan in a very callous manner. It outlaws your right to choose when you die, you are not allowed by law to terminate your life. The state, however, can insist on keeping you alive, even be it artificially. This is why the state gives so much to eliminating terminal illnesses while at the same time prolonging the life of those who are seeking to leave this world through illness. Who is really afraid of death? Death is an inevitable occurrence and as a natural event subjected to Divine law, and should be respected by all. For Spirit, it is as big a privilege as being born.

God gives your body life and also removes that life. The fear instilled in you by church and state denies you the comfort of a happy passing of your Spirit from one form to its real self and real-world, its Spirit and the Spirit World, the home of God. This same fear is the 'tool' used to control every part of your life. This fear is the product of humanity engrossed in its own negativity. The human takes over the God role with the ultimate threat, that it will take away your freedom or even your life, one way or another, should you break its human-made laws. What 'authority' fails to realise is the foolishness it portrays by such threats. If death is an inevitable consequence of being born, and the release of your Spirit is the only consequence of dying, what is there to fear when it occurs, once you are in a perpetual state of readiness?

To be spiritually aware, and live that awareness is to be ready. If you are ready then you can happily live your life to its fullest. If you are spiritually aware you remove the ultimate threat any human can have over you, the fear of death. We say, "Fear not the unknown, for the 'unknown' is with us, and we know. There is nothing to fear."

Spirit – Return into Paradise.

UNRECOGNISED ADDICTION.

Paradise is there for all to re-discover. To find Paradise in your next life you will first need to discover it in your present life. If you don't find it there, how will you know what to look for when you get here. This is why so many who are unaware, on arriving here, look for what is familiar to them and find the 'hell' they have just left, and the demons that haunted their lives on earth. You can now see what we mean.

The first step towards regaining Paradise is to think for yourself. There is no need for a radical or sudden change. There are no shortcuts. The sun doesn't suddenly switch on to lighten your day, it dawns on you. You might think we are just about to enlighten you, to suddenly turn your world into a Paradise, but that is not so. We will provide the words, your thinking on those words will be the process, and your actions on those words will provide Paradise. Paradise will dawn on you, but not without your responsible action. You just have to "pull back the curtains".

You might wonder where do you start? We are delighted to say you have well and truly started your journey. When you asked the question in your mind, when you sought the answer, you discovered these words. When you read these words, you begin to open your mind, you begin to think. As we said, you need to think for yourself. Your thinking up to now has been based on the controlled programme provided by the state and religious structures that are in place, to ensure you become the obedient servant to them. The state makes its own laws to protect itself and religion uses its human-made laws to exert its control over your Spirit. Spirit knows no fear, only your ego fears. The fear of punishment for transgressing the laws of the church or the state is controlling your ego and is effective in that manipulating manner. You look on those afflicted with an addiction of any type with disdain or sympathy, but fail to recognise your own addictions.

The basis of any addiction is the control the addictive substance has over the addict. Could it not be you are addicted to and controlled by the state and the church. You use the church to mould the state and the state to mould the church, while they both use the fear they have instilled in you, or hold over you, to mould you into their requirements. They mould your ego. They acknowledge your academic greatness, but what they are acknowledging is the success they themselves have had in turning you into their slave. Now if you were to think for yourself you would soon realise how unfulfilling that condition is, a 'fool's Paradise'.

As with any addiction, it is important for the addict to acknowledge that they are indeed subservient to the influence of the substance they are addicted to. In the situation we are addressing here, it is important for those who populate and comprise 'western society', that they are, hypothetically, addicted to the substance of the inseparable compounds of state and church. Of course, everything in creation is of God, but under the influence of ignorant and manipulative human egos, anything can become corrupted by the negativity that is so much part of humankind. This negativity is fuelled by the influencing substances. This negativity creates a total illusionary world for the negativity to dwell in and become self-contained. This is why we refer to life in that state as being hell-like, with the principles of church and state being the devils stoking the 'fires'. If you can step out of your addiction for a moment and ponder this scenario. you will allow yourself to see the wisdom contained in these words. If you are to try and throw away, or break loose from the shackles that restrain you and maintain you in that vulnerable lifestyle, how would you feel? Do you feel fear? Do you feel weak? Do you feel exposed? Do you feel unsupported? Let us reassure you that should you ever feel you should become free, there is no need for any of these undermining feelings to be entertained, as God will be your guide, your guardian and your support. God will never do anything for you but will give you the inspiration, the courage, and the strength so to overcome your addictions and become a fully functioning Spiritual Human Being. You have come this far with us, why stop now?

Spirit – Return into Paradise.

CRISES OF CONSCIENCE.

How then is your fear now? We see that you are caught between what your Spirit desires and the desires of your ego. We have also had to live through that experience, so understand how you are feeling. Please ignore this crisis of conscience, for that is what it is. This is the very same as anybody removing themselves from an addiction, their loyalty divided between where they are coming from, and where they are going to. Seeing as you don't really know where you are going, the pull to remain is more than likely the choice you would make. But wait, have you listened to what we were saying? Do you not feel that subtle pull from us, and by what we have drawn your attention to? In your heart you know we are right, that we have come from God, and that your Spirit has called upon us to answer the questions, your discontentment with your life is rising within you.

We will never intrude on your will, and we will be ever-present while you are on your journey. As we have already said this is not a quick fix, it will take time. You will dictate how long it takes, by the actions you put into place. Through this channel, we can bring God to you. The channel is that opened by these writings.

As God can only govern the world that is Spirit, you must enter the consciousness that is spiritual. The spiritual aspects within your physical being are being nourished by the content of these writings. The feelings you are experiencing will get stronger and you will become more confident and less fearful. You will not feel more powerful, as that power is an ego thing, but you will find you are more self-assured and more content to let others find their path, and not seek to follow them. You will establish your own truth and find paradise through that. It will take time but will happen without any physical or mental effort, It will require observation, proper judgement, and the ability to assimilate the lessons that will be presented to you.

You will be confronted by many fears. Remember no test that is put to you is to prove your inadequacies, rather they are put to you to show your capacity to overcome them and that the fears they first evoked were groundless. Think how you must have felt as a child with this world before you. You took on the task of learning all the skills necessary for your survival and well-being. You had humans there to support you, though they too had to be trusted and their way copied. That was for your mind and body self. You as a child were very conscious of us here in Spirit and this gave you the strength and courage to take on the process of growing into the human world.

It is a pity, but nonetheless part of your journey, that you found the world not aware of your true nature, and that did not couple your spirituality to your humanity. The more your body and mind grew the awareness of the real you, you the Spirit, diminished, and also the awareness of true God diminished to such a small scale it was easily overlooked. The physical demands of life took over and the spiritual needs were ignored. No wonder you find life difficult. All that is good is of God. All that is not good is of humankind, ignorant humankind. It is now your duty to yourself to reinstate God into your life. This does not require you to radically change anything other than your thinking. In every situation in your life, for a short trial period, view it from a perspective that you think we might have. Invite us into your life, not as angels or such notions, but as your friends and companions. Invite us to accompany you as you go about your daily tasks. This will in effect turn your life into a spiritual experience. You might even find your human friends will notice your changing before you do, but change you will. It might entail you having to relinquish some very human habits, and this can be difficult, especially where it involves others. Others who resent or criticise your changes are not concerned about how you are being affected but how they themselves are being affected by the changes in you. You might not fit into their circle anymore. In hindsight, you will see that this is a good thing as it wasn't a friendly circle, and was possibly unhealthy.

If you can detach from the abnormal ways of society then you will have time to indulge in the spiritual ways. What then is the spiritual way for the human being? Firstly, to be in harmony within all aspects of itself and then to be in harmony with all that surrounds it in life. Harmony is communication with the Spirit of everything.

Spirit – Return into Paradise.

YOUR CHOICE, YOUR RESPONSIBILITY.

Have you noticed how your day is going? Is it going well, just alright or is it going badly? From where we are your day is the way you meant it to be. It is your responsibility the way it is and your responsibility to make the most of it. You may use the excuse of factors that are outside your control are affecting your day. If you are honest with yourself you will find at some stage in your life you signed up for whatever it is that is affecting you, your happiness and freedom.

We tire, actually we don't but we like to use the expression of the excuses the human gives for having invited trouble into its life. If we go back to the beginning and remind you that you are in that world by choice and your Spirit takes full responsibility for making that choice. Your Spirit chose your parents, their circumstances, and their environment perfectly, for the provision of the life your Spirit required to fulfil its role in the Divine creative process. The tasks presented to you for resolution are so that you can assist your Spirit in this process. These tasks cannot be performed in our world as there would be no evolution here if that were the case.

93

The difficulty you might have in seeing the relevance of this is only because you attempt to see it from your earth-based materialistic point of view. If you were to require some fellow human to undertake an experience on your behalf, you would like to make it as easy for them as possible, and then reward them for their efforts. Spirit does likewise. Spirit works with simplicity, utilising the Law of Cause and Effect. The humans, not understanding this law and being limited by the education, and by the laws of church and state finds difficulty in the expression of our needs and the tasks that are required of them. We are holding the image of Paradise as the potential destination for your life there.

This is a complicated task for you but only because the goal of humankind interferes with your vision. The vision of humankind is very varied so the goals are numerous. Your indecision as to which goal you prefer, with the offering by society as to how you might achieve it, also confuses the issue. The first point of confrontation for the growing human child is when the adult enquires as to what they would like to do when they are older. Because the child is indoctrinated rather than educated, it has very limited choices, that it is aware of. What has this child's uniqueness to do with anything that already exists?

Uniqueness doesn't fit into slavery. So, the future of this child is grim. This is why we have broken from the writings regarding the "Journey through Embodiment". We had come to the point of the child's future years, the years where they will prepare to go out into the world, and what needs to be included in their upbringing to prepare them for the tasks ahead. The goals that are presented to them are so often alien to their purpose. All the training they will undergo to achieve those goals will prove difficult for them. They are introduced to the fear of failure, and the threat of punishment. A divide is created amongst the children, a division of social class, education and career.

The normal interaction between juveniles becomes socially sectarian and divisions and sub-divisions are generated. Often brightness and true intelligence is seen as troublesome and those expressing these qualities are seen as uncontrollable, by the establishment, whereas, they are perhaps more connected to their spiritual purpose rather than their socially generated ego purpose. These juveniles are feared by "upper society" and the power enforcers. Should one become independent they risk being ostracised by those who choose to belong to the cluster of subservient societies that cannot understand anyone who might be 'different'. See how the churchgoers behave towards 'non-believers'. See how society treats those who are differently-abled, see how society treats those who reject the system it offers them in return for their obedience. Neither church nor state is a very good role model when it comes to those seeking a spiritual life. Neither the church nor state will relinquish their grip on society unless there is a radical change in the thinking of those in "power".

Think of the real meanings of the word revolution. Perhaps that is what is needed, the whole world to revolve, but on a different axis. Could that axis not be Spirit. Humankind needs a spiritual revolution.

Spirit – Return into Paradise.

SPIRITUAL REVOLUTION.

There is a certain irony when one talks of revolution, the human mind conjures images of protest marches, sides being drawn, those for change and those for no change, street battles with tear gas and banners, eventually leading to open warfare with bullets and bombs. A spiritual revolution requires none of this chaos. A spiritual revolution has no sides, as such, except aware and unaware. There is no canvassing for members, no difficult initiations, no preaching. It is a matter of consciousness and not conscience.

A spiritual revolution takes place within the human individual and can be triggered simply by opening your eyes. If you are to imagine yourself as God, how would you view this world that humankind has created on your beautiful earth? Imagine how you would have acted if part of your creation had disobeyed you? Would you not think that every day would be seen as your day, as you were its Creator? Would you think you would like to destroy it and start over again? We know how God 'feels' about all this. God, by conferring free will has only to observe and God knows there is an eternity for the situation to be rectified without needing to go back and start again.

The evolution of the Spirit never stops. The evolution of the human species stops, regresses, restarts and progresses to the point where it stops again, and then repeats the process. This is because it is not in harmony with its spirituality. It is the interference of the systems developed by humankind that causes this to happen, and it is happening again unless something or someone changes it. We hope many will read these words and become the change-makers. With numerous individuals becoming aware and changing how they choose to live, though these individuals individually will have little impact, the many sharing a common understanding will certainly make inroads into the corruption created by the unaware and by those who fear change.

Having read these words so far has made you think. We hope that you haven't yet accepted them and still see them as a hypothesis and are pondering on them. When you begin to notice alternatives being presented to you, pause before accepting them and consider what is best for your Spirit. At this time, you will be so engrossed in your lifestyle that your reaction to the spiritual presentation will be automatically negative. It will be necessary for you to consider, and take responsibility for, the decision you are about to make. Will it be spiritually beneficial or spiritually detrimental? This is the first question you need to ask yourself. If you were to meditate on the subject then you would need to meditate spiritually before you will get clear and succinct guidance.

Many spiritual practices have been usurped by ruthless individuals. Many spiritual practices have been commercialised by ignorant people. Why would one think they can improve on perfection? Could it be that they would seek to synthesise spirituality and spiritual practices? Could it be they are seeking to replace God? It is these people that will present a resistance to your revolution. It is their ignorance that is failing humankind. There are too many of these 'gods' in your world, obscuring reality under the banner of 'enlightenment', 'lightworker-ing', psychics, guru, avatar, etc. Amongst this plethora of so-called 'spiritual' servers, there are of course genuine souls who think what they are doing is good when in fact it is not. These souls have been duped by their 'teachers', by those they call their 'masters'. The human world has become so confused by all the different religions, and all the different 'spiritual services' that are on offer. These bogus services are very obviously visible, but the means available for one to recognise them have been conditioned to accept them, by the removal of spiritual discernment from the human psyche. Why so many religions and yet only one God? Why so many people who have a problem with even using the term God and prefer to call on 'the source', or the 'universe' instead. It may be spiritual if it says so. If it doesn't say so then it certainly isn't. As we point out, it may be spiritual, and our reason for saying this is because of the ruthless use of the term, spiritual. By applying this check, it will reduce the number of 'spiritual' offerings that are on the commercial market. Should you seek such a service, just ask us and we will direct you.

There are too many who subscribe to being 'spiritual' for egotistical reasons. Ego and Spirit can be mixed but mixed like oil and water, water being the Spirit, essential to life, and the carrier substance for the oil, together but still separate.

Spirit – Return into Paradise.

THE CONFLICT BETWEEN EGO AND SPIRIT.

Spirituality is a personal and individually unique relationship between the ego and the incarnate Spirit. You, your Spirit is of course a Spirit being and therefore has its own unique place within the complexities of The Spirit. God and The Spirit are One and you, your Spirit, are one with The Spirit, and therefore one with God. It is your ego that is the separate entity and the root of the various dysfunctions that occur during life. Once the ego recognises its place and function, there can be harmony between your Spirit and your ego. The call by many religions to 'surrender yourself to God' is a valid call, except that it has been misconstrued by religion to infer you become subject to the God of that religion, and not see this calling as being addressed to your ego to surrender itself to your Spirit.

If we are to look at the subject of illness, we will see how the conflict of ego and Spirit can not only affect you on a mental level but also on a physical level, not only disrupt your happiness but also your health. You will remember that we have mentioned many times the Law of Cause and Effect, the 'punishment' often given by this Law manifests as illness of some sort. We would also remind you that not all illness is 'punishment', some illnesses are guidance. If one is to take the 'punishment' and use it as guidance then you will see how fair and just this Law is.

Again, we must look at the misrepresentation by religions of this Law. Some use it as an excuse to preach 'Hell and Damnation', others to place blame on the offender and their offence. Spirituality, which is not a religion, sees this Law as providing the opportunity to change, and indeed as the opportunity for an excuse to other people for the need for change, the 'illness' no longer allowing certain behaviour or living. Illness need not only affect the physical body or mind but may manifest in a material sense, such as loss of occupation or some such loss. You will notice how even the severest of illnesses can be experienced and recovered from by using it to invoke change, provided it is the right change, one that comes from within you, inspired. In this way, the 'curse' becomes a blessing. All comes from God and is good.

Once it becomes the possession of the ego it can manifest its goodness or become bad. Only spiritual awareness can ensure you avoid this pitfall. Your ego will always empower your negative side. Unfortunately, the only way God can attract your attention is when all seems hopeless. Your ego will drive you further into the mire it has guided you into. Your Spirit, however, will endeavour to attract your ego's attention and guide you to a point where you can be assisted. It will always require you, the ego, to realise and admit to the dilemma you are in, and also to be open to our guidance. This is especially important when you have all the other avenues open, that your ego has led you into.

In the case of illness, it is very often found that one's delay in opening to Spirit, allows their body to become so damaged that serious intervention becomes necessary, like surgery, and even then, if the recognition of the guidance is still ignored, the illness can become terminal. Of course, in many cases, the illnesses were necessary to encourage the ego to relinquish its hold on the body and permit it to pass away. The eventual outcome always depends on the ego letting go and 'letting God'.

EGO.

Spirituality is a twenty-four-hour activity. This might appear like another strange statement on our part, but when you think of Spirit having no time nor need to rest and that spirituality is unlimited in any circumstance, then you might begin to understand. Think also of what this spiritual state can do for you while you are in spiritual consciousness. You must find all this very confusing while you are experiencing mixed consciousness.

We draw the attention of your ego consciousness to the allure of being part of infinite 'power'. Power is something egos seek. The degree of power any ego has is solely in relation to how it sees itself, and that power is therefore limited, as the ego cannot imagine anything beyond the material world as being achievable. So, we use the bait of infinite 'power' to catch the attention of the ego. Everybody has psychic 'power', and this is part of the ego. If you like it is the tangible, material part of the human ego. The human is the only species in creation to possess an ego. This ego is what makes the human-animal the most dangerous part of the animal domain, indeed the most dangerous part of creation.

Most humans think their way through life. But with their thinking being limited and controlled by church and state, they are controlled by these same systems. It is a human ego action to react to any suggestion that they may be controlled, and that is the cleverness of the controlling or controller. A point worth noting is that humanity is not being controlled by whom or what it thinks might be controlling it. It is not a human or group of humans that are in control. Yes, there are those in power who exercise control over states or religions, but who or what controls them? The answer to the question is, that they are controlled by their egos, and furthermore, their egos are controlled by the great collective energy of negativity, sometimes called the devil or referred to as evil. This collective negative energy is also a twenty-four-hour activity. The human is a subject of this negativity constantly, unless, the human is spiritually aware and spiritually conscious. Negativity will constantly oppose positivity, particularly when the human consciousness hovers between being ego or Spirit consciousness.

It is a phenomenon of human psychosis that the psychotic often become religious, and often fanatically so. Such is the power of religious delusion. However, should the psychotic person become aware of the control that is held on their lives and rebel against that while in the delusional state, mayhem can manifest. Their mixed consciousness explodes into total inexplicable chaos, that is unless the spiritual side of their nature is treated with love, understanding and shown compassion. However, the usual solution is to medicate them into insensibility, by anaesthetising their ego. This is, if you like, why often those who trade on their natural psychic abilities become, in themselves, deluded by their ego and can even become psychotic.

SOUL CONSCIOUSNESS.

It is interesting how humankind brands negativity as 'evil'. Has it not become obvious that as everything in creation is of God, then surely positive and negative must also be from God, and part of creation? If we truly look at creation and see all the components in it as positive, as they are God-given, then how can negativity be considered to be anything else but also God-given, as it exists within God's creation. Nothing in God's creation is other than positive, and everything in creation is there for the benefit of each component. The Spirit in every component is also part of God.

Because you are in the flesh of a human, and in the human environment where all your apparent needs are met by the social structures around you, it is easy to lose sight of God and God's goodness. These writings, for example, are to help you realise and address the absence, or presence, within you of your Godliness. They are also to highlight what it is that is obscuring your vision of the true God. You are heading towards the Light. The symbolism in the rising sun of every day, and how it draws you from the darkness; the symbolism of the night, and how it gives you time to rest. How there are creatures of the day and creatures of the night. How all creatures, night or day are affected and controlled by the light of the sun, and instinctively head for it or head away from it. Their instincts, the instincts that each component of creation possesses, are there to serve the incumbent Spirit on its personal journey. The symbolism of the sun again, as it continues on its journey, passing behind clouds, its light being obscured behind something, sometimes shining in all its glory, playing chasing with darkness, and yet always bright and somewhere, ever-present; the symbolism of the ever-presence of God. Then how can you ever think you can be in permanent darkness when the Divine Light is always there, somewhere? It is up to you to find it and enjoy the comfort it affords you.

It is your fear of the dark that releases the demons of negativity. It causes doubt, especially when it is used by others to frighten you. Neither soul nor Spirit can ever physically harm you, so why would you fear. They can, however, by their desire to remain in a state of soul consciousness, and depending on their acquired awareness gained through their journey through life, be either in a 'negative' or 'positive' state. The soul consciousness is but the remnants of the ego generated during the lifetime. In other words, had they lived a positive life and gained the awareness of God, they will be in a positive state. On the other hand, had they failed to find God-awareness in their sojourn in your world, then they will have fear and be in a negative state. In the world of soul consciousness, there is a manifestation of good and bad, good souls and bad souls. It must be remembered that both these souls have their Spirit still in situ. The Spirit cannot vacate the soul until the soul becomes purified. Those who pass into the soul world in a state of spiritual awareness are already purified but might decide to wait until those they were related to by the bond of love also return to that soul state. These aware souls might also stay at that 'level' to help those loved ones who still remain on earth. The

Spirit within the aware souls can leave the soul state and enter the Spirit world at will.

If you take these communications as an example; at the beginning we mentioned how we were Webb, Sebastian etc. These would have been the incarnations we had experienced. To communicate with your consciousness at that time we had to become one with the soul of that time, we had to become one again with that consciousness and converse with you at that level. As your awareness developed, we were able to gently raise our consciousness and also raise yours, until we could return to the Spirit world and continue our conversations from here. It was a difficult process for you as you needed much protection from the incursion of souls that were unaware and still in their ignorance. These would have been constantly at hand. You would have experienced momentary fear. This fear would have been generated by those souls and had you succumbed to those fears, you would in effect have become open to their influence. Thankfully we had gained your trust and thus decreased the likelihood of that happening.

When in an incarnate state you feel fear, there is a chance that negativity is about. If you become fearful, it is due to a lack of awareness of, and trust in God, and those of us who help God. Many have received so much misguidance from those who pose as God's messengers or helpers that it makes it difficult to trust that God even exists. That is why they look constantly for tangible evidence, and this is what religion provides, but only evidence of their God's existence. You have their God's temples, their God's ministers, and their God's angels. All religions subscribe to the existence of a 'Supreme' God, the father of the one they hold as theirs, but yet hold theirs as the one to be revered and followed. If there is only one God, and most religions agree on this claim, then who are all the others that they refer to as God? There is only one true God who can also be called The Spirit and in essence that is what God is. Like you, the true you, in essence are Spirit, a part of God.

Spirit – Return into Paradise.

YOU CALL THE CHANGES.

Many people struggle with the thought that they might have to change their view of their world and that they might also have to change their lifestyle. There are no sudden changes needed. Again, we stress the simplicity and uncomplicatedness of spirituality. Your awareness will call for the changes, when and if necessary. You will find that you will reject what was once attractive to you. You were attracted to whatever that was, as a replacement for the lack of spiritual satisfaction and nourishment from your lifestyle.

These compulsions that many experience, such as the need for food outside of mealtimes, and indeed the need for excessive food; the need to drink alcoholic beverages to quench one's thirst; the need to pollute one's lungs with tobacco smoke so they feel they can relax; the need to take any form of a hallucinogenic to cope with the life they are choosing to lead, are triggered by a form of hunger. This hunger is really a hunger for change.

Unfortunately, there is little in your world that will attract the necessary awareness that will allow the victim of this hunger to identify what is an opportunity for real fulfilment. Some turn to religion and cling to their beliefs in the hope that they won't sink.

Religion, in this instance, is like a lifebelt that will eventually become sodden and begin to sink. The victim will cling to that lifebelt and consequently will sink with it. This is why, with religion, it may have the language but it lacks the substance, it lacks the Spirit. It is also unfortunate that religion can turn people from spirituality.

If you think of times when you felt truly fulfilled, you will remember times when you were in a state of mind to be close to your Godliness. There are other times when you spoke from your heart, and that felt good. There are also times when you know you are being truthful to yourself. All these times it was the feeling of goodness, and inwardly the feeling of Godliness. That's the fulfilment. Other times when you eat your food, remember we spoke of this earlier, well-produced, prepared, and cooked food needs little garnishing, it is full of love. When you eat this food you also get that feeling we are referring to in this conversation.

If we are to expand this concept into every activity in your day, how many of your 'doings' would give you that feeling? If any percentage of activity lacks that sense then it also lacks the inclusion of the ingredient called God. God takes up no space in your life when you are God aware. Initially, you might find it necessary to consciously bring God into your daily life. The training often received in God matters is that God only gets one day in your week. As we have said spirituality is a twenty-four-hour process, and every day also, and all your life. Eventually, as your spiritual awareness increases, and you adapt to being a spiritual being, everything you do in life will be for the Spirit within you and therefore for God. There has been talk of the 'second coming', surely this is it, the awareness and practice of spirituality, of Godlikeness and Godliness.

THE TIME TO DIE.

They say, "time passes quickly when you're having a good time". Many in your world fear growing old, not a fear we have in this world. Growing old is a natural part of the physical process. It might be some comfort to those who are experiencing this ageing process, that it is part of the consideration that Spirit applied when they choose the body to incarnate into. They assess its durability to succeed in achieving the spiritual results that they would require from that lifetime.

Under the Law of Cause and Effect, you will never die before your time, no matter how long or how short your life may be. When you are on course for your Spirit's journey, you will find time will appear to pass very quickly, and when not on its course, it will drag by. Look how quickly your holidays pass and how slowly your working days pass, unless you are working within your vocation, then time will pass quickly, that is unless there are unnecessary interferences in your employment that control you exercising your spiritual 'duty'.

We have spoken regarding how the opposition to positivity is negativity, and how this is something that will constantly be present in your life, presenting its negativity to every positive action you may make. We have told you how negativity needs no invitation, and that positivity occurs only when you evoke it. Could we recommend to you, that you place beside your bedside a reminder for your awakening, that you determine to invite your coming day to be a positive one, and never to concern yourself with the thoughts of the ever-presence of negativity? Negativity, at its worst, can only place obstacles in your way, positivity is in how you overcome them. The 'punishment' under the Law is how you succumb to the negativity and give in to it, long dreary hopeless days, and the 'reward' is how your days get better and better, and pass quickly, through the love of God.

The duration of your life is no reflection on whether you are leading a 'good' or a 'bad' life. However, how you feel about the speed at which life is passing can be. We have also spoken about the fear of dying. Many are so afraid of dying that they refuse to die, and can prolong the process unnecessarily, and often painfully, both physically and mentally. You will notice how one family member dying can quickly lead to another family member following them, as if the first passing had reassured the other, helping them to also make that transition. That is often the case, and often the significance is missed. All deaths deserve to be celebrated, even though at times they appear to be unexpected or undeserved. Death is always through the achievement of life's spiritual purpose, even though it might not suit the ego of the dying body or the egos of those who would even seek to deny the body the right to die.

Modern medical science is ego-based and lacks any real element of spirituality. It mostly concerns itself with the prolongation of life, and the extension of suffering, and then seeks to minimise the suffering with further pills and potions. Most illnesses that humans suffer are acquired through inappropriate behaviour and /or lifestyle. Most human lives exceed the spiritual usefulness of the body and its environs. If there was no fear around death you would experience many people dying at a lesser age. The longer living people would still be fulfilling their spiritual duties by being the elders within the community, the history carriers, and the carriers of wisdom on to successive generations.

Please never forget that the purpose of life on earth is for the expansion of spiritual awareness within the realms of Spirit, of God. Earth life is never for the benefit of humanity. Humanity is but a biological process developed and developing to serve the needs of God. If you like, it is God's laboratory in the continuing process of creation. We see many opposed to the theory of evolution. It may not be exactly as others have seen it, but all are evolving nonetheless, at least spiritually. All the rest will physically evolve to accommodate the evolving needs of the Spirit.

Spirit – Return into Paradise.

YOUR LIFE IS FOR YOU.

Many feel that life is harsh for them. To those, we would say that it is the life they chose and if they feel it is harsh then they need to ask themselves why they chose it to be that way. We cannot stress enough that whatever way you are experiencing your life it is as a consequence of, (A), choices your Spirit made prior to your birth, and/or, (B), choices made on your behalf by those you chose to take responsibility for you until you could take care of yourself, and/or, (C), choices you have made since you reached the age of reason and the age of responsibility. Whichever way it is, it is your choice and responsibility.

Naturally many compare their life to the life of others, a foolish trait, since the life of another may be very different but nonetheless equally of the same value, experientially, for their Spirit as your life is for your Spirit. Every moment in your life carries a message for you and about you. You might think that others who control your life have to carry some blame for how difficult yours is. They didn't ask you to come into your life so they could control you; it was you who chose to be in their life and you who accepted the invitation to join them as such.

The real pitfall is your ego and how, when it gains control, will 'sell' itself to the highest bidder, sometimes at a great cost to its own self-esteem and confidence. Your ego needs to be loved and appreciated, your ego needs to be fulfilled and your ego needs to be nourished and fed. Your ego is constantly foraging for its enhancement and will place itself in any position that will provide this. Should its choice fail, the ego will never accept responsibility, if it succeeds then it will grow and expand but it's all an illusion that the ego is suffering. But then this is the human life, a life devoid of spiritual awareness. The ego can even convince itself that it is humble. Spirit recognises 'enough' whereas the ego only recognises 'more'.

Most things in the human world take precedence when they appeal to the ego. Many people avoid the truth and settle for the comfort of belief and ignorance. They find the truth too heavy a burden, such is their ego illusion. It's easier to live with the consequence of a lie than a consequence of the truth, this is what we see the humans preferring. If you look now at the harshness in your life and how it is orchestrated by you, by your choices and actions, by your ignoring the truth, by you not taking responsibility, by being egotistical, by being selfish and greedy, by deflecting the lessons that the Law of Cause and Effect are offering you, ask yourself then, 'could life be any other way?'.

IT ALL COSTS MONEY, SELLING YOUR SOUL.

Let us have another look at humanity and the many structures it is now subjected to. For you to have your own place to live your life within, you have to purchase it. You are controlled by the ownership of others. An interesting question is where did the vendor acquire the rights to ownership in the first place?

In the beginning, God created all that there is in your world, with love and without condition. God didn't create the property that was placed on the land, God created the land itself. This land is for the use and benefit of all that God created. It is there for the trees to grow, the grass to grow, the animals and insects and birds to grow. It is there to be shared by all, and not to be fenced off and hoarded for the singular benefit of an individual and to be sold for material gain. In the very act of artificial portioning of the land, humankind defies God for personal gain and to feed its own ego.

If you like, this is the beginning of your entry into servitude. To purchase the land to live in and perhaps to build your own structure, you again need to recognise your servile position. You have to register your purchase and then apply for permission to build. Every transaction will incur costs. In your world, the energy of payment is called money. Where does this money come from, unless you earn it? How do you earn it? You have to become subservient to an employer. Even if you are self-employed, you will have to supply some service to someone who has the money to pay you for your time. The time you sell them is the time you could spend building your house, but then you can't build your house without materials and materials cost money. Where do you get money, you earn it? So, you are now caught in the spiral of servitude so that you can access that which God has bequeathed to you, through God's creation. You are not allowed, under the present structures of society, to live the life that is natural to you, that is if you can even know what is now natural.

This is where Paradise lies hidden, covered up by the deceit perpetrated by what some might call high society. It is a shame that many in your world seek to aspire to that type of society, to that corrupted use of this wonderful being you are. It is a very high price to pay to feel proud and to have your life achievements marked by the wealth and material goods you have earned the money to pay for. Why then do so many feel valueless? There are those who have nothing, except the skills required to live an affordable life, those who have the courage to shun the temptation of materialism, and perhaps to flaunt the man-made laws that are only designed to keep them in slavery to those bullies who call themselves masters.

Materialism can never satisfy the hunger for Spirituality, and neither can religion. Slavery is not the answer either. Freedom of thought and freedom of life is the only way to Paradise. There is another way, other than that offered by your society. Unfortunately, your worth is measured in money earning potential. It is a pity that your earning potential is determined by how well you are prepared to accept the life your society offers you. You will have been reared with stories of the temptation of the 'devil', for 'devil' now use the term 'social system', it is the social system that now imposes so far into your life that you are either in it or outside it, that system has made it virtually impossible to survive outside it.

Our solution is simple. Remain within the system but use it instead of it using you. Develop your integrity based on spiritual values. Listen for the Spirit of the oppressor, and not listen to the ego. Be aware of the word 'have' in any conversation, especially if it is implying that you are the one who is being directed by it. It is always your choice, or at least should be. You, after all, are the one who will bear the consequence of obeying the demand. Are you prepared to accept that?

Spirit – Return into Paradise.

YOUR VOCATION.

The past unresolved is always there to catch up on you. Unresolved, or better still, not fully utilised, it lingers behind you on your road to fulfilment. It drags on you slowing your progress and often stops your progress altogether. When you become complacent around its existence is when it is at its most dangerous.

No doubt these writings will provoke some unpleasant memories from your past. In doing so, these writings allow you to address those issues afresh; only for the reason of helping you resolve them. We have spoken so often of responsibility and would remind you that everything in your life to date has been there through your choices and therefore are your responsibility. We know this can be very hard for anyone to accept, but only if they are ego controlled. Spirit sees that everything happens for a good reason, the ego determines whether it approves or disapproves, determines if it is 'good' or 'bad'. The reason why there are unresolved issues in your past is that you sought to solve them from an ego perspective. Forgiveness is no remedy as it is an ego undertaking and is generally used to escape the real message of the spiritual guidance and learning contained in the event. Once you can have a full understanding of the scenario, then you can assimilate its lessons into wisdom for your present and apply that wisdom to your future. In this way you can continue your journey unimpeded, going from adventure to adventure.

If there are things you are aware of that you have not done, do them now. It's never too late. Assess where you now see yourself. Ask yourself are you fulfilling your ambitions or did you just happen to make it this far in life? Remind yourself of your childhood dreams about growing up. Do those dreams have any relevance to where you are? Had you forgotten them or discounted them? Were they dashed by the influence of others or other things and events? Often you were more aware of your future when you were a child. Have you ever noticed how many receive what is often called a late vocation? This vocation is normally what they would have intended all along, had they been aware.

How many people upon retiring from their work begin to study fresh subjects? Many do, and also take up a hobby that they would normally not have had the time nor finances to follow; the man who wanted to be an engine driver when he was a child but became a doctor of a banker or some such instead, because he thought he needed the money. In retirement, he drives trains for some preservation society and wishes he had done that earlier. Where is your life at these times? How is your vocation doing? How much control do you feel you have over your life? Are you happy? If you weren't doing what you are doing, what else would you see yourself at?

USING THE 'FLOW' OR JUST DRIFTING?

We asked you many questions during these discourses, how many have you tried answering? We also told you that you needed to ask yourself these questions as your motivation needs to be constantly monitored for ego awareness. If you tried to answer us it would indicate that you are not taking life seriously, and seeing it as something you have to do for some reason or other. That then would also be indicating that you are not living responsibly and that you are only biding time until you die. Yes, you might feel that you have accomplished much so far in your life. What you no doubt have had are many experiences, and survived them, which we suppose would be considered, in your terms, an accomplishment but if it is that you have not assimilated the positivity of the lessons contained in those events, then you have accomplished very little.

One cannot simply go with the flow, which would only take you to where the 'flow' wants to deposit you, and not necessarily the destination that your Spirit is seeking for you to take it to. Too many drift along with the flow of life being obedient to the requirements of the society it was born into, never questioning or addressing their spirituality and the spiritual purpose in this life they have chosen. When we questioned you, it was so that you might question yourself. When one asks a question, it is because they think they haven't the answer, and on getting the answer they often find they already knew it. Of course, sometimes they didn't though their ego won't let them admit it. If you felt that we were questioning you to see how aware you are, that also would be the case, but we won't answer you or judge you for not knowing the answer. The answer will come once you create the circumstances to permit it. You won't get the answer if you think you already have it. The answer you think you have is also the wrong one if life has not thought it to you.

We have confused you, however, all will become clearer as we go along. You have many concepts that spiritually are obstructive. You raise questions to us that are really irrelevant. For example, you ask, "Why is the world in such a terrible state?" The answer is it is in that state because you (humankind) have caused it to be. You have the answer, not us or God. Our world is Paradise, remember?

You constantly interfere in the lives of others rather than seeing how things are for you and understanding how they got that way. If you were to occupy yourself with your life and see everything around you as being relevant, all being part of your personal creation, you wouldn't have time to be bothered by how good or bad others might be doing. You have too many distractions, too many worries that keep you distracted from looking to see where you are and where you are going. This life will need your constant attention. Remember when you prepare for sleep, consciously switch your mind into 'Spirit mode' so that during the hours your ego is inactive we can adjust your 'program'. This adjustment is a spiritual exercise, a spiritual service that will help you to be more aware when you wake in the morning.

Spirit – Return into Paradise.

TIME IS ONLY A CONCEPT THAT HAS IMPORTANCE TO THE HUMAN.

We spoke of spiritually obstructive concepts. Another obstructive concept that is in the human world is the concept of time. Humankind only needs time measured in days, hours and minutes so that it can allocate certain activities to certain times. You have work time, leisure time, and a time we frequently hear called 'no time'. Even 'no time' is obstructive in so far as it is a time that nothing can be done. We hear the expression though, 'I'll have that done in no time', and often we see it taking 'forever', and never getting finished. If it is finished in 'no time' then it is surely rushed!

Humanity has 'languaged' time in a very peculiar way and has consequently confused itself with its own language. You will hear the accusation of being 'early' or 'late'. Who or what determines this? Yet people get there 'as soon as they could' but are still 'late? The one setting the time has set it to their convenience and seldom allows for Devine intervention. A financial value is attributed to your time by society which determines how much your time is worth to them and not by how much your time is worth to you. Have you ever thought about how much your time is worth? How often have those words been uttered around the death bed, "I only wish I had more time", and "I'd give anything for more time". Time is only a concept that has importance to the human, every other species is unconcerned about what time it is. All of creation knows spiritual time, it's God's time, a time set in Creation and by the Law of Cause and Effect. You can let time pass you by but you can never kill time. When your life comes to a stop you never stop living, not even when you die. Now is always the right time. The right time is when everything that is meant to happen at that time happens. Time is never too long nor too short. The end is never the end as life is eternal and doesn't depend on embodiment alone. Your world needs time as it has devised it as a control mechanism. Time is invaluable to humans but not in a spiritual sense. No money can buy time, that is God's time, and is not for sale. So, you see how time is in a spiritual sense and how it compares in a material sense.

We have said it is spiritually obstructive. We say this because we see how your society has given itself more time and only allocated a small part to religious practices. Some say their prayers in the morning and some at night. Some pray at mid-day and some at allocated times during the day. The majority of time in your world is devoted to serving the body through toil of some sort. The human has devised many systems for doing this. These systems only serve to maintain the 'lords' and provide the serfs with the minimum in return for their time. The system has found a way of buying and selling God's time as it has found a way of buying and selling God's land.

You are the custodian of your own time, the time provided through the advent of your creation. You have chosen to be born into that world and into that body. That body's timescale has been converted into a human time scale with every moment of its life marked in some way by the years, hours and minutes of its life. The time to be born is set by the incarnating Spirit, as is the time to die. No man can set those times. Remember life begins with the incarnating Spirit entering the body, and life ends when it departs and starts its homeward journey. The period between these two events is your time.

You can choose what time to sleep and what time to wake. When others set your time scale you need to set an alarm to wake you. Why do you think you need to be 'alarmed'? Why do you choose a lifestyle that requires you to be alarmed so that you awaken? Looking at this from our perspective is it any wonder that we need to 'alarm' you to get you to awaken to your Spirit's needs? We present you with situations like illness to draw your attention to more important matters. We present situations to you that 'ring' alarm bells.

The only reason you suffer fright or fear is that we have awoken you from the apparent comfort of your life to the reality of the reason you are on that earth. It is then that your time seems to have been cut short but by our terms has reached to perfect time for you to raise your consciousness to your true spiritual purpose. Take some time and think about these words.

Spirit – Return into Paradise.

EGO MIND.

Do you organise your life? Are you in control of your life? These might sound like strange questions and your immediate response will tell you that they require consideration. A mind that is under the control of the ego will provide a spontaneous reply of "of course" to both. A mind under the control of Spirit will ponder and continue to question itself. The egoist will respond immediately and the spiritual person will ponder, and might not even see the need to reply at all.

The ego-mind is full of conflict, fear, confusion and doubt. It never really knows what is right or what is wrong for itself or for anything. The ego-mind will probably be living in the mind of another, trying to live life through them. The ego-mind will try and control others and not realise it is under the control of many sources, the state, the church, the darkness, and of course its own personal negativity. For many people, this is the way their life is. They are not bad people, but they may, in extreme cases be people behaving badly. Look around you. Is the world you see the way you would want it to be? How would you change it and why? Why would you even see the need to change the world? Remember we said that it is as you need it to be.

If you would seek to change the world you are denying your input into it becoming the way it is for you. We are sure you will find this difficult to accept and that you will find many reasons outside of yourself to blame for your predicament. Now, look at the world without the luxury of being able to exonerate your responsibilities and blame the world, and even God for your dilemma. You will now see the world in a different light. You will see a world full of challenges, and also mistakes. You will see a history that leads up to this calamity, a confused history, a history full of contradictions, a history with so many viewpoints that the truth has been lost. One thing that hasn't been lost is the results of the past. The result of the past is the present. What matters history now? If you can keep your focus on the now and accept all that is in your life and deal with that, then you will be on the road to minding your own business and on the path to spiritual success.

This is simplicity. You will find you do not need to change the whole world, and realise you only need to change that one little bit you occupy, taking control of your life, you organising your life for yourself and your way. Only you know how to do this. You will need though, to go to the top of this current discussion when we asked those questions. Who or what is controlling your life? Is it your ego or your Spirit?

SPIRITUAL CONSCIOUSNESS AND EGO CONSCIOUSNESS.

One must constantly question the decisions one makes, verifying the source of inspiration behind those decisions. There are many factors that can influence your choices. Choices are made by the human side of your consciousness but this can be inspired by your Spirit. Your Spirit will never seek to control you, that is, it will not take 'control' until asked by your ego to do so. Spirit never takes control as such, it will only inspire, and the control remains with you.

There are many 'layers' to your consciousness, though for this exercise we will break it into two major compartments, the spiritual consciousness and the ego consciousness. In the spirit-consciousness, your only influence is from your Spirit and from God, one and the same. In your ego-consciousness, there are many influences, all emanating from the indoctrination you received since your birth into that world. There are so many influences 'shouting' out instructions as to what you should do, or what you have to do, that it is almost impossible to hear the subtle whisper of your Spirit. Spirit influence is generally felt rather than heard or seen, though sometimes can be 'seen' through the symbols that are presented in life experiences or in dreams. Spontaneous responses or decisions are normally from the ego-mind and are most often regretted. Spirit needs for you to make 'space' in your mind for it to give you the guidance you seek. However, once you have become aware of the correct balance, that is when your ego becomes aware of its sharing this life with your Spirit, you will hesitate for just a moment to consider your options, and then you will make reasoned and balanced decisions and choices.

The normal educational facilities of your world do not give you this opportunity. Your society calls for you to act in one way, and your beliefs expect you to act in another way. Your experiences, which are contained within your ego, also call on you to respond to your circumstances in an egotistical way. Poor you, you are being pulled in every direction. The one influence that is not pulling is spiritual influence perhaps that is why it is so often ignored. Of course, it being of Spirit it does not pose the fear or threat of punishment or retribution of some kind should you decide to ignore it. It is only religion that threatens 'hell's fires' should you choose to ignore its instruction or the state that threatens you with monetary fines or incarceration if you defy its ruling. So many in the past have been punished for doing what they thought to be right, though it broke the laws of state or church. God never judges you nor punishes you. The Law of Cause and Effect that some call Karma, will always provide you with the indicators as to the appropriateness of your decision, by rewarding you or allowing you to suffer the consequences of your actions. One way or another you will learn, it is a "kill or cure" system, sometimes literally.

Nothing threatens your Spirit and this is why in making choices in life it can provide you with the best guidance. All it needs is for you to give it a chance. In time using this method for arriving at decisions will put you on your true path, and become a way of living. Once you achieve adulthood, you will have become more accustomed to living by the rules of humankind even though they might contravene what you understand as spiritual laws. Spirit has very few laws for you to contravene, other than the primary law as we have already discussed. It is often thought that the punishment for sin is waiting for you when you leave that world, but it isn't, you will already have 'paid' for your transgressions before you leave. You might not have learnt from the offensive experience and subsequent repercussions. If you haven't learnt positively through your experience you will remain in ignorance. Should you pass from that world you will still be ignorant and bring that ignorance into the world of soul, or purgatory as some call it. You are still Spirit and still trapped inside the ego, trapped by its ignorance. This is also an important part of the Spirit's experience. The ego is still in control and is still behaving ignorantly, doing what it ignorantly thinks all souls should do. This ego still thinks it knows better. The Law of Cause and Effect still applies. Some poor ignorant souls think it is their duty to continue to 'sin' and suffer, and rattle chains to attract attention to their perceived power or plight. Of course, others lead an exemplary life, by religious standards that is, but they are still spiritually unaware and think that because they have left the earth and still feel they are alive, they must be in heaven, and seek to go no further.

We look after all these souls in any way we can. In much the same way we look after you if you let us. We cannot do anything for them, but we can guide them to doing for themselves. We can guide you the same way by giving you these words, increasing your awareness of the forces acting for you or against you. It is up to you how you choose to listen and implement this inspiration in your life. It is always up to you.

COMMUNICATION WITH SPIRIT IS NEITHER A 'GIFT NOR A 'POWER'.

Communicating with Spirit beings is a relatively simple task, most creatures do it constantly. Watch your pets as they perceive the presence of a Spirit. The difficulty that most humans have is their ego's quest for power, the quest for exclusive recognition. You will hear Spirit communication referred to as a 'gift', or as a 'power' that someone has. It is neither a gift nor a power. We have told you this many times before and repeat it here for inclusion in this dissertation. Communication with discarnate beings only requires awareness. The 'level' at which the communication takes place is an entirely different matter. We spoke previously of 'levels' of consciousness. In the reality of spiritual consciousness, there are no 'levels' of consciousness. Perhaps it could be termed more conscious or less conscious.

In the ego world there are certainly many grades of consciousness, none of which include spiritual consciousness. Spiritual consciousness is contained within the soul body or envelope that protects the Spirit. The soul body allows the influence of Spirit to enter the physical being, but only when the ego permits it. It could be said that the mature ego which has not been raised with spiritual awareness is unaware and unenlightened, and to all intents and purposes asleep. The ego body will need an event so difficult for it to explain as anything other than an epiphany, in order for it to wake up. It will often seek to explain away the event saying it was a coincidence, that it was someone else's fault, they might even suggest it was imagined and didn't happen. Yet these same people will go to someone who poses as a medium for advice, and with some ruthless readers that's what they will get, their vice added to.

We have said that communication with Spirit is simple and two-way. You can address Spirit directly and Spirit can direct you equally easy and the proviso is always if your ego allows it. The ego will readily permit soul communication, this is done using the psychic senses of the human. The danger of this practice is that the soul realm is where negativity and positivity co-exist. As we said the consciousness of the 'medium' will determine whether they access the consciousness of soul or of Spirit. Unfortunately, so many are prepared to be satisfied with their communicating with souls. This is a very useful service and can lead to communicating with Spirit but not many persist with developing their awareness that 'far'. It is similar to someone studying for a profession. The full course might take many years before completion, but some only stay long enough to learn the language, and then start to practice without completing the course or having the experience. Would you trust someone who has this meagre training? Would you put your life in their hands? Many only spend a weekend or two training to be a medium and think because some soul came calling that they are now a medium?

Spiritual consciousness is not acquired by attending a course and learning techniques. Most courses offered in this way are ego training and little more. They can show you what you are capable of and what is natural to you, but they can never teach you spirituality. It is very difficult to teach someone what they already know. The proper course will help you realise your innate spiritual ability, will help your ego become aware of your Spirit, and by educating the ego enable your Spirit to access and influence the environment your body enjoys. It is natural then for you to 'see' and 'hear' Spirit, it is also natural for your body to become a channel for the Divine energy to flow through. It will be natural for you to then live your life spiritually and knowingly.

Be aware of the pitfalls that the egos of others prepare for you. Others who recognise your spiritual progress might find it intimidating and seek to restrain you rather than to accompany you. The egos of others will constantly seek to reduce your consciousness to their 'level' rather than aspire to raise their consciousness to the 'level' of yours.

Spirit – Return into Paradise.

THE CORRUPT WORLD.

It is all too reminiscent of the past for us to look at the world of humankind as it is now. Many times humankind has reached this degraded moral and ego ridden status, where corruption and disruption of God's creation has been defiled by the greed of the few. Unfortunately, there is no justice in the consequences of this travesty; all have to bear the brunt of the Law of Cause and Effect. On the brighter side of what could happen under these circumstances is that the degree to which this will affect humankind is proportional to the awareness of the individual and how they chose to bring that awareness into their lives.

Many think that it is sufficient to be aware, but if that awareness is infested with laziness and lacks the motivation that is the Spirit within the human then it is not spiritual awareness and is but intellectual awareness. In other words, it is only an egotistical awareness and therefore not spiritual.

Many suppose they are spiritual but that is because they tell themselves that they are. Because one proclaims they are on a spiritual path, doing 'spiritual' things, behaving in a 'spiritual' manner does not mean they are spiritual. The reason your world is in such an unbalanced state is because of these senseless suppositions. No one can call themselves spiritual, we cannot call ourselves that and we are pure Spirit. As you evolve spiritually, as you become more spiritually aware, you will begin to realise that you are not able to do this, to call yourself spiritual. The suggestion that you are spiritual suggests that you have arrived at the destination of your journey and that you have achieved the purpose for your life on earth. We have said to you before that we are all still on that journey, that it's an infinite journey, so how can anybody think they have reached a conclusion?

To think one is spiritual only shows the deception of the ego. The ego can be satisfied with words, the Spirit is satisfied with action. One cannot call themselves spiritual but they can live in a spiritual way, and yet this doesn't make them spiritual, at least not in their own eyes. You need not see confirmation that you are spiritual from any other source either as this again would be your ego seeking notoriety for itself. The Law of Cause and Effect will give you plenty of notice of where you are with the way your life is going. If you are happy you must be doing right by what your path might be, if you are unhappy then you must be in the wrong place and doing the wrong things and all for the wrong reasons. Now isn't that simple? Why would you keep doing what is creating your unhappiness? Why do you resist the changes that can assist you in becoming happy?

We started this period of writing by saying how corrupt the world of humankind had become. It has become thus with the collaboration of many generations of humans and has reached this degraded state through the 'successful' structuring of your social system. Humankind is imploring God for change to occur and then awaits the hand of God to intervene. If humankind does not realise that it is themselves that needs to change then Divine intervention could take place and humankind would be annihilated. However, if some have the awareness of Spirit and the way of Spirit, they would take such a conflagration in their stride and instinctively know what to do. At this moment in time, many are aware but not sufficiently strong to allow their awareness to manifest. Yes, there are those who would ridicule, or chastise the spiritual one and for that reason, many remain hidden and spiritually inoperable. The controller is fear and this fear is assisted by a lack of trust in God. Many are afraid of repercussions for their highlighting the malpractices occurring within their communities and this allows for the corruption to continue and grow. Remember the old adage, "Things only get as bad as they need to get in order to invite change". How bad are things in your world now? Why not speak out? Why not change yourself first? If you do not speak out then you have no right to speak. Irrespective of what others do you have an obligation to yourself, and to those you love, to do something that would make you happy and fulfilled. It is up to you to do the right thing for yourself and this will automatically influence others to follow suit, hopefully for themselves.

Things are reaching a critical stage globally in your world. There is still time for change to occur. There are the embers still glowing after millennia and the breath of honesty will fan these embers into bright flame, purging the world of humankind of all the dishonesty and corruption that is so prevalent today. Your world needs you to stand up and get doing what you came to this earth to do, to get to know and to see God and to show the world that you are doing it for yourself. You will be that ember, let the Spirit enflame you. God bless you.

SPIRITUAL MEDITATION.

You will have gathered from the tone of our previous communication that another has joined us here. So that you will understand, these communications come from a 'level' of consciousness that the receptor can access, and in turn, we can access a higher 'level' in accordance with our ability. At times, therefore, we defer to a communicator from 'higher' still, and this is where the previous communication emanated from, in other words from a place closer to God. Now let us continue.

As was said spirituality is an activity and not a state. Knowledge only becomes spiritual knowledge when that knowledge is acted upon in the interests of the Spirit. What one culture sees as a sacred practice another culture will take on as a pastime. We would refer you to the practice of smoking tobacco, a sacred practice to the Native Americans but a habit in the western culture.

All of creation is sacred to the spiritual mind, yet how we see it is constantly desecrated by Humankind, especially in western society. There is very little taught to the children regarding respect for nature and to respecting one another. We see how bullying is so prevalent amongst humans, bullying of children by other children and indeed by ignorant adults. We see bullying by the system's members of its own members. We see bullying by the political class upon the voters. We see the bullying by the so-called servants to the public of the people they are supposed to serve. We see religious bullying of the followers of that religion, and we see the believers of that religion bullying the none believers. It is very hard to find peace, love or harmony in your world. It does exist but not where you would traditionally expect to find it. It exists in a part of the minds of the human, a part rarely exercised or referenced. It is in the spiritual part of everybody's thinking. The part of the mind the average consciousness is unconscious of.

This is the part of the mind that generally has to wait until the physical mind quietens. This is where this communication resonates. This is where you go when you practice spiritual meditation. This is the part of the mind that Spirit will use to communicate with you through. The more you exercise this part the better your spiritual activation will be. When you spiritually meditate it is best to meditate in a facilitated and non-intrusive gathering. All ego must be left outside of the sacred meditative circle, and this includes the ego of the facilitator. The reason why a facilitated meditation group is so effective is that the participants do not need to be so disciplined and can more easily surrender to their Spirit under the guidance of the more experienced 'leader'.

There are no rules regarding how this should be carried out, other than the safety and comfort of the body needs to be addressed so that it is not distracted by any discomfort during the session. A good facilitator will often assist you in your relaxation and your confidence in the facilitator will allow your body to give itself to the process also. Don't look for any particular experience from meditation. Looking for anything is keeping the physical mind conscious and does not allow the spiritual mind to come forward. We hear of people 'sitting for development'! We wonder what they are seeking to develop other than awareness.

Spiritual growth is a natural process. Like anything seeking to grow the growth program is already there and is awaiting the signal to grow. This is what Spiritual meditation is about. Your choice to attend such a group is your Spirit inspiring your body to attend and your subsequent attendance is the signal for the program to activate. Spiritual meditation is time you set aside for the sacred practice of nourishing the spiritual growth, the growth in spiritual awareness of your body, of your ego, so that it may prove to be a good transporter of your Spirit through its life on earth. With this company of a well-balanced body-mind and Spirit-mind, you will always find happiness no matter how miserable you may appear to be. Your Spirit is always jubilant in these circumstances.

Spirit – Return into Paradise.

EPILOGUE.

These writings were given to me in 2018. Little did I know what Spirit had in mind for the world. In the process of editing these words for publication in 2021, I now realise that it was the current pandemic that was being forecast. In these writings it can be seen why such action was needed, the guidance it is to give us, and the actions that will bring about the necessary changes required to save humanity and the world.

Brendan.

Spirit – Return into Paradise.

Also in this Series…..

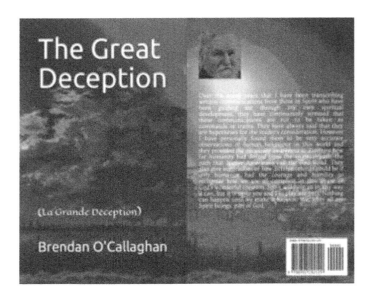

All these books are available from your nearest **Amazon** store.

Just type my name into the search bar.

Made in the USA
Middletown, DE
24 July 2022